CBT SKILLS & PRACTICES WORKBOOK FOR SELF-ESTEEM

FOSTER AN AUTHENTIC LIFE WITH AN IMPROVED SENSE OF SELF-WORTH, CONFIDENCE, AND INNER STRENGTH BY OVERCOMING SELF-DOUBT AND MANAGING SELF-CRITICISM

MARTI MCCOY

FREE BONUS

101 Affirmations To Boost Your Self-Esteem

Free

Scan with Your Camera to Join in

CONTENTS

INTRODUCTION

"You're in your own head."
"You're too harsh on yourself."
"Cut yourself some slack."
"Go easy on yourself."

These common statements are a pointer to a bigger inner process. They point to how you speak to yourself.

Everyone has an inner voice. The inner voice, however, is different from person to person. In some, it is a harsh critic, while in others, it may be the voice of a loving parent.

Your inner voice is very personal. It will sound different depending on the situation. You could be tolerant with yourself in certain circumstances but harsh in others. In some people, the inner voice could be more thought than an actual voice. In others, it could be a clear, personified self-communication.

Your inner voice differs mainly in intensity and tone. It also shifts depending on your awareness of what you are saying to yourself.

In this book, *Cognitive Behavioral Therapy (CBT) Skills and Practices Workbook for Self-Esteem*, we will develop a comprehensive strategy by which you can foster an authentic inner life.

The inner life builds the outward life. The benefits of an improved inner life include an improved sense of self-worth, higher levels of confidence, and inner strength or fortitude.

Behavioral therapy skills will work for you as an individual. If you are reaching for improvements in career, in business, or your relationships, a grasp of the cognitive therapy skills we will discuss in this book will help you to overcome self-doubt and take strides where you would previously have either procrastinated or even talked yourself out of taking action.

The book will also serve as a companion to the behavioral therapist who seeks to help their clients to develop greater levels of confidence and self-worth.

Self-criticism is like being in a toxic relationship with a partner who never lets up. They keep talking and talking and talking. Yet nothing they say is constructive or encouraging. They find fault in everything you do. Such an inner voice breaks down the sense of self from within and shows its effects in the decisions and choices the individual makes because they second guess themselves.

You can identify some of the tragic effects of low self-esteem around you. Notice the gifted individual who never seems to rise above mediocrity. Take time to observe the attractive and loving young person who keeps falling into abusive relationships. Listen to the highly intelligent individual who keeps abusing one substance or other.

You will observe the effects of low self-esteem in the business person with astounding success factors, but who is always teetering on the edge of business collapse because they keep making terrible choices.

Sometimes it will be the highly qualified professional, unable to come out of their comfort zone to reach for greater career rewards. They give themselves reasons why they do not deserve the good things in life.

That is the overall inner conversation of low self-esteem. Wherever it rears its ugly head, low self-esteem robs the individual of the good that could be in their life. They underperform even when they can accomplish so much more.

They miss out on the best life events, beautiful relationships, amazing opportunities, and practically anything that would have made their life beautiful.

Low self-esteem reduces the best among us to a life of being average and mediocre. Often, the victim will not only be completely regular, but they will go a step further to actively sabotage themselves.

This is why Cognitive Behavioral Therapy (CBT) skills are so essential. They empower the individual with skills to take charge of their inner space effectively.

With CBT skills, the individual moves to being one who achieves the goals they set for themselves. They start to dare to become more, do more, and ultimately, even have more.

For the therapist, this CBT Skills Workbook will help you gain some of the most rewarding encounters in your career. You will have a front-row view of the transformation of your clients. You will watch the individual come into your practice bowed down and bent on self-sabotage. They will drag themselves in, look down at their feet, and mumble answers.

You will watch the same individual transform into a person who stands straight, holds their head up high, responds to matters with clarity, and has a spring in their step. You will watch their eyes move from being shifty and listless to being filled with good humor and life.

CBT skills are an effective way to help people to become the kind of person they are happy to be.

I am excited to be your partner in studying the skills in this book because I know what they can do. I was that person who, not too long ago, walked with a shuffle, bowed down, and was more likely to sabotage my own progress. That was before I understood the immense importance of learning to work with the inner voice.

I learned to hear my internal arguments and get a sense of whether the argument I was putting forward was for my benefit. Was I defending a weak position because I was afraid or because there was something I needed to do differently?

I learned to understand my internal distortions. I am not saying that my inner dialogue is now always perfect, but I have gained perspective and the ability to shift what was going on within me to support my goals.

The other benefit I gained from mastering CBT skills is improved relationships. As I understood myself better, I could also understand others much better. In important personal relationships and in business, I gained a better grasp of other people's motivations. In time, I was better equipped to develop methods to cooperate with them, resulting in more fulfilling relationships.

An unexpected yield of my appreciation of CBT skills was that I found ways to cope with difficult situations. Previously, I would get stumped by challenges, withdraw into myself and let the problem fester until it was too big to deal with. This way of coping with challenges was frustrating and made me lose many wonderful opportunities.

I did not like the results I was getting in my life, and I know many people who struggle with low self-esteem are very unhappy with their life results too.

That is why I have developed this book as a workbook. It offers problem-solving strategies that are practical and relevant to your specific situation. This is not a theoretical book. It presents workable skills you can use for life. You will know how to map where you started and see the results you make over time.

Behavioral change is not a mere theory. You can see the transformation, even if you might start completely unaware of what your inner voice sounds like, how it makes you feel, and what you can do to change it.

The primary outcome of this book is to help you appreciate that you have an active and ongoing relationship with yourself. You build that relationship through many years of talking to yourself in a certain way.

This book is about helping you to develop a more uplifting and beautiful relationship with yourself. You will identify what your inner conversations do to you and how they affect your decision-making process.

As you start to identify the difference between your thoughts and your inner voice, you will see just how deeply you influence every experience you have as an adult. Most important is that you will gain the knowledge and skill to become a better friend to yourself.

By the end of this book, you will be quite familiar with your inner voice and will know when you are in your own head tearing yourself down. Then you will not need another to tell you to cut yourself some slack. You will be the one telling yourself that you do not need to be too harsh with yourself.

As you develop an inner friendship with your inner voice, you will have found ways to motivate and empower yourself from within. You will have methods and go-to skills to face your fears so they do not overwhelm you.

Your moments of panic and overwhelm will consistently reduce, and in time, you will be the smiley person with a life that is working for them.

So let us start learning right away.

You are ready for a wonderful journey of discovering CBT skills.

1

INTERNAL MONOLOGUE

There are days you wake up feeling great and positive. It feels like the whole world is your canvas and you are invincible. You believe you will accomplish and be successful in the things you set your heart to do.

There are other days when everything looks bleak. You don't think anything will work. You are discouraged and frustrated. The slightest setback gets you deep into feelings of worthlessness.

If you struggle with low self-esteem, then the bad days are more than the good ones. You are tired. You feel as though you are constantly fighting a losing battle. Any small matter that does not work out as it should causes you to feel even more dejected and frustrated. You feel depressed and are constantly battling with feelings of anxiety.

These are not strange feelings. You can overcome these feelings. You can improve your inner world to a place where you have more good days than bad days. The first step in this journey into a more uplifting life is to identify where the problem begins.

Most people believe that depression, anxiety, and feelings of frustration are responses to what is going on in their lives. They interact with family and the conversations leave them feeling uncomfortable. As a result, they tag family meetings as the source of the problem.

Others have bad days at school or work, so they tag that activity as the source of their negative feelings. This cannot be further from the truth. The way your life unfolds has a lot more to do with your thought patterns than with the events of your life. Let us find out more about your internal monologues.

WHAT ARE INTERNAL MONOLOGUES?

Three factors interact within all of us. Our **thoughts** cause **feelings,** and our feelings impact our **actions**. This is called the *"cognitive triangle."* It is the interaction between our thoughts, our feelings, and our actions.

The cognitive triangle is derived from the works of Dr. Aaron T. Beck, who introduced the concept in behavioral therapy in the 1960s. It remains a key anchor for CBT skills and forms a basis for the effectiveness of therapy tools. The cognitive triangle demonstrates the interaction between the individual's thoughts, feelings, and behaviors.

Internal monologues is a term that amplifies the thoughts and conversations that go on within us in this triangle of cognition. In his timeless work, *"What to Say When You Talk to Yourself,"* Dr. Shad Helmstetter captures the impact of internal dialogues or self-talk beautifully.

"After examining the philosophies, the theories, and the practiced methods of influencing human behavior, I was shocked to learn the simplicity of that one small fact: You will become what you think about most; your success or failure in anything, large or small, will depend on your programming - what you accept from others, and what you say when you talk to yourself.

It is no longer a success theory; it is a simple but powerful fact. Neither luck nor desire has the slightest thing to do with it. It makes no difference whether we believe it or not. The brain simply believes what you tell it most. And what you tell it about you, it will create. It has no choice."

— DR. SHAD HELMSTETTER

In ordinary circuits, talking to self is oftentimes considered a sign of a mental health problem. In behavioral therapy, internal monologues are a significant factor in overcoming the effects of low self-esteem.

We should mention here that if the voices within the individual get so loud to the extent that they start to respond to them loudly and as though they are a real person, then they may be having a problem. Talking to oneself loudly and with hand motions as though one is speaking to another may be an early sign of certain types of brain disease and neurological conditions. These, most often, will require psychiatric intervention.

In most people, the inner monologue is not necessarily an audible voice. It is thoughts, but with a back and forth component to make them a tangible influence on behavior.

Internal monologues are also referred to as internal dialogues in some works. This highlights the idea that an internal dialogue often has two sides as though two people are carrying on a debate within the individual. The most common internal monologue is a discussion where you are both the speaker and the respondent, but all in your head. You make a proposal and you defend it or trash it. You give yourself supporting reasons to do something and at the same time give yourself reasons why doing what you wish to do is not such a good idea.

In some people, internal monologues are so compelling that they have a personality that is just as real as another human being. However, people with such strong internal dialogues are very aware that the other person is a part of their own mental discussion and not an external party.

The earliest evidence of internal dialogue is with children. When a child plays alone, they sometimes speak audibly to themselves. In their play, they will be both the initiator of an idea as well as the voice of the parent who counters the idea. They can even be two children, yet they are alone. Internal dialogue is not an abnormality.

As we grow older, the audible dialogue becomes silent, but the internal dialogue remains and becomes a commentary within the individual and in everything they do.

Some people respond to stressful situations by developing an active inner conversation. Inner conversations also support learning. You may find it easier to retain information if you have memorized it and speak it quietly to yourself later.

Music and songs stuck in the mind are also a type of inner monologues. They take on a distinct emotion such as joy or sorrow, depending on the emotional response you associate with the song.

The most important aspect of evaluating your inner monologue is identifying how it affects your emotional life. What kinds of things do you tell yourself?

Practice:

This week take time to listen to how you think. As you go about your day, listen to this internal monologue going on within you. In some of us, it is an almost audible voice. You can identify it. You can tell the age of the voice. You can assess if the voice is angry or happy with you. Start to identify some of the ten most common things you tell yourself.

THE POWER OF INNER DIALOGUE

Young people internalize faulty monologues that can cripple their potential. Yet it is not just young people. If harmful internal monologue is not captured and adjusted early enough, then the adult also continues to speak to themselves in ways that harm their self-esteem and eventually, their ability to be effective.

Let us take an example of a young adult who grows up as a third child in a home of five children. As a middle child, they often felt ignored. In most homes, the older children get attention because they are expected to step up and guide the younger children. The younger children get attention because they are young and need more care than the older ones.

A young person growing up between their siblings in such a home may develop a way of thinking where they tell themselves they are never good enough and that is why they never get attention. Although it may be true that they do not get attention, they have given a wrong reason for it. The parents were not deliberately ignoring them. It could just be that they were not old enough to be recipients of the demands made on the older children, and were not young enough to get the care that the younger ones required.

This young person is now an adult and they are going about their business. They get a good job, but they always feel ignored. They have taught their mind to misinterpret not getting direct attention as an indictment against them. They tell themselves such things as:

"No one ever notices my efforts."
"No one sees how hard I work."
"Why do I work so hard and try so hard and no one cares?"

Meanwhile, it is quite likely that they do not get attention at work because they are good workers and do not draw attention to themselves.

In time, if they continue to tell themselves that no one cares whether they work well or not, they may start to make mistakes and leave things undone. They start to give less in the areas that were their responsibility. The longer they give themselves negative feedback, the lower their performance becomes. In time, they start to get the attention they desire, but for the wrong reasons.

The inner dialogue now changes to:

"People always pick on me."
"When I make the smallest mistake, it is noticed. Yet when others make bigger mistakes, no one says anything."

They fail to recognize that they draw more negative attention because they are capable, but are performing below their ability. The low performance attracts negative attention from management.

The more the individual continues to yarn the wrong thoughts around their experience, the worse their relationships at work become. In time, they may very well get fired, which then plunges them deeper into negative internal monologues.

Internal monologues are powerful because they influence the way we see the world.

They also affect one's sense of self or self-esteem.

The young person who kept thinking that they were ignored at home because they were not good enough will evolve to tell themselves that they cannot perform well in life.

If such an individual gets into a relationship, they will add new aspects to the negative monologue and systematically drive people away. No one enjoys spending time with a whiner. Even worse, no one enjoys spending time with people who are unappreciative of the efforts of others.

Individuals who have told themselves that they are never noticed will not appreciate positive attention when it comes to them. They will distort it to mean that they received attention for a completely different and usually negative reason.

For instance, rather than appreciate the attention they get from a loved one, they will say the loved one was trying to manipulate them, or something equally absurd. They will always find reasons to negate positive attention, because they have taught themselves to only expect negative attention or no attention at all. When they get no attention, they will distort the lack of attention too.

This is how inner monologue affects self-esteem. The more the individual anticipates negative attention or feedback, the deeper they go into feeling worthless and inferior.

THE IMPORTANCE OF YOUR INTERNAL MONOLOGUE

Following the example above, you will see that internal monologue can build or destroy your life. It is difficult for many people who are inclined to having negative internal monologue to accept that there is a lot of positivity around them. When an individual has learned to cling onto negativity within their inner dialogue, even the best events in life take on an ugly and negative hue.

At the beginning of this book, we said our most important task is to help you become your own friend.

Mental health conversation has taken center stage in many parts of the world. With the proliferation of such information channels as social media, TV, and entertainment out of Hollywood, more people are inclined to question their life experiences.

After growing up entertained by the attractive and beautiful lives of Hollywood characters, it is quite natural for many people to ask why their lives are not as amazing as the lives painted in the movies and in books.

Social media platforms, as is the norm with all staged photography, tends to show people in their best light. The need to appear at one's best has led to such technologies as photo filters and Photoshop that create a false sense of perfection.

Yet we all know that life has a lot of flaws and very few perfect moments, if any.

Friends in Hollywood are perfect, supportive, and never misunderstand a conversation, unless it is an absolutely hilarious misunderstanding. That is not true of real life. Friends are not always supportive and many conversations go off pretty fast unless we are very keen on our communication skills.

Family holidays are fun in books and movies, yet we all know that holidays with family are the times when all our insecurities find the greatest expression.

The disparities presented between our lives and the common media channels that fill most of our restive hours are a major reason why we must consciously pay attention to our inner monologues.

If your internal monologue supports the idea that your life is not up to standard because it is below the standard set by entertainment and social media platforms, then you may start to feel very uncomfortable.

How you speak to yourself sets the stage for how you see yourself in relation to the world. It defines how you see your world, and determines how you interact with others in your world.

Your internal dialogue is deeply important.

THE TWO SIDES OF NEGATIVE MONOLOGUES

There are two sides to the value of our negative internal monologues.

On the one hand, there is a reasonable level of negativity that enables us to cope in a world that can be hostile and unfriendly. For instance, if you are going to cross a busy street, the idea that the driver in the oncoming vehicle will not see you is not only healthy, it probably will save your life.

Some aspects of negative internal conversation is a self-preservation mechanism. In relationships, it will help you identify people that may not have your best interests at heart. In evaluating your performance, there is a healthy element of learning from your mistakes. In such situations, your objective evaluation of your performance, including your mistakes, is important.

When tackling your goals, negative self-evaluation is the difference between complacency and high performance. You may use your inner monologue to demand more of yourself without demeaning your wins.

Therefore, it is not necessary that a person be all flowers and blossoms within. An element of self-preservation is important.

On the other hand, negative self-talk becomes a problem when it turns against you. When you start to be the center of your negative feedback without a balancing appreciation of the positive, then you are treading on dangerous ground. There is a big difference between being your worst critic and being your best one-man support team.

Being your worst critic means you hardly ever give yourself a break. You are always in your own face. You are at the center of reminding yourself how low your performance is when compared to anything and everyone else. Being your worst critic is teaching yourself to be your worst friend.

How You Talk to Yourself

How does your inner dialogue make you feel?

This is the basic self-evaluation question to pose to yourself concerning your inner dialogue.

"I've learned that people will forget what you said, people will forget what you did, but people will never forget how you made them feel."

— MAYA ANGELOU

This is true of others.

It is true of yourself.

How do you make yourself feel? Do you end your day feeling like a total loser or do you believe you did your best and hope that you can do better tomorrow?

The answer is in how you speak to yourself.

You may speak to yourself as an angry critic, or you may be kind to yourself. How you feel about yourself, about your world, and how you feel about others will evolve from how you speak to yourself.

A deep sense of self-hatred will evolve out of constantly stating just how awful you happen to be. Statements such as:

"I am a horrible person."
"Why can't I just be kind to others?"
"What is wrong with me?"

Such self-denigration is counterintuitive.

You can be aware that you could have been kinder or more loving to another. However, a closed statement such as, *"I am a horrible person,"* leaves you no room to negotiate the position. You have locked yourself in with your own words.

By the same token, *"What is wrong with me?"* suggests that there is something wrong with you. It asks the brain to give you reasons why there is something wrong with you. Is it true that there is something wrong with you?

If there is indeed something wrong with you, is it a fixed way of being? Is there anything you can do about it? Is it entrenched in everything you are or is it a learned way of being? If it is something you have learned, can you see the possibility that you can learn something different too?

Self-denigration almost always will degenerate into self-hate. An individual who hates themselves, who sees themselves as a horrible person, has given themselves no room for self-improvement.

The worst of it is that they are always with themselves. Picture yourself in the constant company of not only someone who hates you, but who does not miss a moment to remind you that they absolutely hate you.

That is why negative self-talk will crush even the best of us from within.

We have painted the picture of the power of self-talk, so we will move to the next step: *"What can you do about it?"*

Practical View

Use the questions below to guide your practice of developing your inner monologue.

- At the end of the day, do you feel great or terrible about yourself?
- What are the ten most common things you have heard yourself say to yourself?
- If you were speaking to a friend, would you tell them the same things you tell yourself?
- If you were to become a better friend, how would you change what you say to yourself?

In the next, chapter we will delve into the development of self-esteem.

2

DEVELOPMENT OF SELF-ESTEEM

We dedicate a chapter to the topic of self-esteem because other words come up in the discussion about how we view ourselves. A good grasp of how to assess your self-esteem will help you see why all the other problems resulting from low self-esteem affect your life.

Other common terms are used interchangeably with self-esteem. Such terms include self-image, self-worth, self-confidence, and self-assurance.

They, however, are components of self-esteem and are a part of a healthy sense of self.

WHAT IS SELF-ESTEEM?

"Esteem" in the Online Merriam-Webster Dictionary is *"the regard in which one is held; especially, high regard."* We can deduce then that "self-esteem" is the regard in which an individual holds themselves.

In the Online Psychology Dictionary, *"self-esteem"* is *"the degree to which the qualities contained in our self-concept are seen to be positive. It reflects a person's image of theirself and their accomplishments."*

Self-esteem is the way you objectively view yourself, how you have learned to see yourself over time and in relation to your abilities and accomplishments.

Over the years and in the development of theories in psychology, self-esteem has received a lot of attention. Some theories focus on the development of self-esteem, while others dwell on the impact of self-esteem on individual performance.

Famous psychologist, Abraham Maslow, in his psychology classic, *The Theory of Human Motivation,* includes the development of self-esteem in his famous hierarchy of needs. In his definition, he describes self-esteem as one of the main and basic human motivations on the path toward self-actualization. He describes the need to build self-esteem as a factor in personal growth where the apex on the hierarchy of needs is self-actualization.

Self-esteem is a judgment of self. It is an ongoing internal evaluation of self but also a static evaluation of yourself and based on how you assessed your performance in specific circumstances in the past.

You may have accomplished something important to you. In that case, you evaluated yourself highly. You believed in your abilities then. If later you are met with crippling failure, you may not assess yourself highly in that circumstance.

You may take a single aspect of your life and evaluate yourself against the performance of others. If you evaluate yourself and find inadequacies in yourself, then in that instance, you devalue your sense of self. Your sense of self and view of your accomplishments in context will not be too high. You may, however, excel in an area that others do not excel in. When that happens, then you may evaluate yourself highly and in comparison to others.

These fluctuations mean that self-esteem is not a static self-evaluation. It shifts over an individual's lifetime. What we are mostly concerned about in developing and understanding self-esteem is your overall self-evaluation of yourself. If your overall evaluation of self is positive, then all other principles of self will be positive.

COMPONENTS OF SELF-ESTEEM

High self-esteem incorporates a sense of self-confidence, a stable sense of belonging, and a general sense of security in your relationships. Positive self-esteem means you are sure of your place on the earth and have a healthy sense of personal identity.

All these factors together develop into a firm sense of personal competence. The individual believes in their competencies. Where they do not have the necessary competencies, they are not afraid to reach for new knowledge to improve their performance. They do not evaluate the circumstance in which they are not competent as a time to feel inadequate. They use that situation objectively and as an opportunity to learn something new. They feel they have what it takes to learn the new skill or competence.

A person with high self-esteem likes themselves most of the time. They believe that they deserve the good that comes to them because they are worthy of that good. They will not shy away from reaching for more in life because they have assessed themselves and decided that they deserve more, and it is okay for them to want more.

Why Self-Esteem is Important¶

As we have seen, self-esteem is largely a self-evaluation. For this reason, self-esteem will be lowest in childhood, will increase in adolescence, and will grow to a general and overall sense of self in adulthood. If a child grows in an environment that does not support positive reinforcement of their sense of self and abilities, then rather than self-esteem growing in their adolescent years, it drops. By the time the individual is an adult, they will have internalized a negative sense of self, will doubt their capabilities, and generally have low self-esteem.

Since self-esteem also contributes to how your inner monologue evolves, it will affect your decision-making. Self-esteem is your inner self-motivation for those days when things are not going as great as you would want them to. It is your way of reminding yourself that one moment of failure does not make you a failure for life. In this way, you are able to inspire yourself from within. You give yourself inner courage to tackle new challenges.

Positive self-esteem also gives you confidence in your personal and interpersonal skills. Personal skills include how you look, how you dress, and your communication or self-expression abilities. When you are sure and secure in yourself, you are more likely to make better choices choosing your clothes.

The self-confident person does not depend on external attributes, such as a deliberately hideous dress sense, to shock people into accepting them or giving them attention. They are comfortable showing up dressed in clothes that complement their physical attributes. They do not go out of their way to hide behind clothes and make-up. They show up as they are and are comfortable in that appearance.

Self-expression is an important aspect of success. We all need to communicate with others to get ahead. Positive self-esteem helps individuals to express themselves without second-guessing their presentation. They present information clearly, assured that they are communicating well.

They also perform or do better in relationships.

The person with positive self-esteem will express their hopes, aspirations, and desires better in a relationship. The most important relationship is the one an individual has with themselves. The person with positive self-esteem has an uplifting relationship with themselves. They are their first friend and other friends come as additional connections. As a result, they are able to maintain a healthy relationship with another because they are confident in that first relationship with themselves.

Development of Self-Esteem

As just mentioned, self-esteem is at its lowest in children, improves as they move into the teenage years, and it is at its best in adulthood if the individual develops in an optimum manner.

As this conversation is about the development of self-esteem, let us see how an individual might end up with low self-esteem. What factors would be at play in those developmental stages that will affect the way the individual eventually assesses themselves and their abilities?

There are many experiences that a child goes through over the 21 years of development into a young adult. In those developmental years, many people impact the way the child will view themselves either in an instant or for a long time.

Everyone has experiences that will influence the development of a positive sense of self and other experiences that will hinder the development of a healthy sense of self. Most of those experiences will come from guardians, primary caregivers, and educators, while others will come from peers. These are some of the experiences that affect the development of self-esteem.

1. The Critical Parent or Guardian

Some people grow up with a guardian, or for younger children, a primary caregiver, who already has a self-esteem problem. Such an adult around the child will tend to see the ways in which the child makes them feel bad rather than how their inner monologue is affecting their life results. They will tag the child as the source of their distaste and may increasingly hold the child in disdain.

In an emotionally healthy individual, external events are not the primary way through which they evaluate the meaning of their emotions —as such, said external conditions and circumstances, even when pleasant or unpleasant, are not used to give meaning to or dictate how they feel. When they feel positively or negatively in a situation, the individual is aware that their *interpretation of the situation* and circumstances is why they feel the way they do, not the events themselves.

They often view life events and then choose how to respond to them. They, therefore, will not find a child in their care an irritant, a bother, a disturbance, or a trigger for other negative feelings. They will view the child from the position of an adult who has a child in their care.

This is to say that not all adults with the role of primary caregiver, parent, or guardian necessarily have the same sense of self. The lower the sense of self is in a guardian, the more they tend to react negatively toward the child. Such responses will often be unhealthy and evolve into faultfinding directed at the child.

Unfortunately, the words spoken to the growing child find a highly absorbent mind. The child will take in the criticism and end up describing themselves in equally harsh and critical terms.

Listen to your inner dialogue. If your inner monologue takes on the same tone as that of a critical caregiver, we will be looking at ways to adjust that voice so that you are not a captive of someone else's negative opinion of you.

2. Children Can Be Cruel

Children tease one other at play. Not all children come from the same homes and not all families share the same standard of what is cruel and what is acceptable. Therefore, what one child may consider casual play may be hurtful to another.

Also, one child may come from a home where they are incessantly criticized. Such a child as described in the previous point, has parents or guardians who are harsh and cruel to them. What may be friendly banter from other children may further harm a child already struggling with a poor sense of self.

The third possibility concerns naturally shy children. Such a child may not look forward to the easy banter that goes on with other children of their age. If such a child receives unusually harsh criticism, they are likely to think it over long enough for the idea to take root in their minds as a pointer to who they are.

Whatever the circumstances, there are children who have negative experiences from the words of other children they interact with. Some children deliberately harm other children in school or at play because they are bullies.

There are many reasons put forward as to why a child becomes a bully. In an interesting turn, most bullies also tend to be children with a very unhealthy sense of self. Their self-esteem may be low for various factors. Children who are different, for instance, may be teased by their peers. To protect themselves, they turn into bullies, pick on other children, and turn others into sport.

3. Deliberate Physical and Emotional Harm and Abuse

A child under attack by an adult or an older child who is significantly stronger is a victim. If such an attack is recurrent, then we are looking at a case of continuing physical abuse.

There is no justification for violence, especially not against a child who cannot defend themselves against such an attack. A child who has experienced physical abuse will internalize the harm and convince themselves that had they been better, the adult would not have assaulted them. As already mentioned, when the internal monologue is distorted, then the individual develops a faulty sense of self.

When a caregiver, parent, or guardian gains sexual arousal, pleasure, or satisfaction from a child, then whether it happens once or several times, that adult is sexually abusing the child.

As in physical abuse, the sexually abused child develops a distorted sense of self. To begin with, they consider it their fault that they were sexually appealing to the perpetrator. They think they are the ones that warranted the attention they received and if they had just been less conspicuous, or less attractive, or dressed differently, or been a completely different child, then they would not have received the sexual advances.

Abuse, be it sexual or physical, harms one's sense of self because their internal monologue becomes distorted. The line between the facts and the justifications for the harm are blurred enough to cause the individual to maladjust in the way they see themselves and the world around them.

Within a family setting, an abused child is further compelled to either tell a lie or to behave in ways that will protect the abuser, further distorting their view of people and of themselves. Abuse, whether within the family or from an adult close or well known to the family and to the child, will negatively impact the development of the individual's sense of self.

4. Poverty, Neglect, and Unpleasant Circumstances

When life takes too much away from some, they tend to internalize the extreme lack of basic resources as a sign of their inadequacy. Some of the factors that lead to low self-esteem include the constant inability to accomplish basic tasks because of an extreme lack of necessary resources.

A young person who is constantly out of school because the parents or guardians could not afford the fees will see that as a statement on how little they can accomplish.

Parents or guardians who neglect children, including children given into their care, will also hinder the healthy development of self-esteem in the child.

5. Social Media, Entertainment, and Other Factors That Trigger Unrealistic Expectation

As already mentioned, mass media, social media, and entertainment channels provide a view of life that is perfect and whole than it is in reality. The standards set in such communication outlets are intended for entertainment and are deliberately crafted to create a false reality. They are supposed to be an escape, not a standard for how life should be, but try telling that to your brain.

These media portray actors with the perfect figure, height, weight, skin tone, etc. They will have pre-defined circumstances when they are within a different social and economic background, which may not always be an accurate representation of reality. It is practically impossible to capture all the deviations of life in movies and entertainment. There has to be some level of bias.

A child who grows under the direct influence of productions that portray perfections or unneces-sarily grand imperfections, as the case may be, gets the subtle message that they are inadequate. This feeling is exacerbated if the child does not fit the given standard of body size, shape, height, skin tone, and social background presented in such productions.

Additional technologies and social media platforms that encourage sharing of perfect looks and perfect moments increase the need to be that perfect person. Body shaming in all its forms is a toxic development in human history. It allows bullies and mostly insecure people to make others feel hurt and generally inadequate.

If the individual under such an assault has a low self-esteem as a result of any one of the earlier factors, such online bullying can completely destroy the individual's sense of self.

GROWING UP IN POSITIVE NURTURE

In a perfect world, all parents, guardians, and educators would aspire that all children grow in an environment where they are appreciated and validated. Children who develop a healthy sense of self grow up in home and school environments where they are heard. They learn to believe in what they have to say because the adults around them allowed them to speak.

They also have adults around them who show respect for one another and love to the child. Such children learn that they are worthy, celebrated, and develop a healthy sense of self. This is not to suggest that only those who grow up in ideal circumstances have a healthy self-esteem. Children who grow up in favorable conditions have a higher potential to develop a healthy sense of self, but everyone can work on their self-esteem.

A less than adequate environment is not the end of the road for one's sense of self. Even if you currently have a poor sense of self, you can develop healthy self-esteem with specific interventions. Additionally, even children who grow up in ideal circumstances can develop unhealthy self-esteem. Such influences may come from other factors outside of school and the home, such as the company a child keeps.

Parents with mobile careers may find their children unable to build stable relationships as a result of having to relocate constantly. This inability to bond with others or the recurrent broken bonds will make the child susceptible to forming unhealthy friendships. Such friendships may affect their sense of self.

Self-Esteem Influences That Come Later in Life

For the most part, we have discussed the development of self-esteem in children and adolescents. However, even adults with healthy self-esteem may encounter circumstances that affect their view of self.

Poor health and physical impairments from disease or accidents are major reasons for a drastic shift in how an individual views themselves as an adult. For a person who was healthy and had no physical impairments, an accident, a crippling disease, or being in constant pain can and will affect their view of their abilities.

Marital challenges, conflicts with a significant other, separations, and even divorce can leave the individual feeling like a failure. This is especially true for people who had built their sense of self around a particular accomplishment; in this case, getting married and living happily ever after.

Turning a decade and growing older has a negative impact on some people. This is particularly common if the age change also comes with either an economic downturn or a health problem.

Social challenges such as racial discrimination in a new environment or where the individual works or lives can also affect one's sense of self. The challenge with such social issues is that the individual is bombarded with slurs and innuendos frequently enough to cause them to start to question who they are.

Practical View

Your self-esteem is the way you evaluate your worthiness and abilities in life.

- How do you view yourself and your worthiness in life?
- Do you believe you are worthy of the good things that come to you?
- What are the factors you can identify in your life that are influencing the way you view yourself?
- What are the specific areas you would want to improve? List them as we will tackle them in the coming chapters.

In the next chapter, we will discuss in detail the issues that arise with low self-esteem and how to ascertain that one's self-esteem is in danger.

3

LOW SELF-ESTEEM IS LIFE-THREATENING

Why should we care about self-esteem?

Manifestations of low self-esteem show up in most mental health disorders. That is alarming enough on its own. A healthy sense of self is the foundation for a productive life. For the child, a healthy sense of self will enable them to build meaningful relationships and learn effectively. For adolescents, it helps turn their attention to productive activities rather than self-destructive ones.

In an adult, a healthy sense of self will enable you to accomplish your goals and live up to your potential. Without it, most people tend to slip in and out of anxiety more often. In many cases, they will slip into depression and maintain unhealthy and destructive relationships.

A healthy sense of self enables a person to pay attention to their own well-being. They prioritize self-preservation.

Low self-esteem is a life-threatening issue because, when unchecked, it eventually develops into tendencies toward self-harm.

SELF-ESTEEM IN MENTAL HEALTH DISORDERS

Low self-esteem will be present in therapy patients who manifest anxiety and depression. It will show up in patients who have challenges with substance abuse, who tend to be violent, who are suicidal, and in those with eating disorders.

Low self-esteem is common in individuals who have battled substance abuse and anxiety for some time. Some people are genetically wired to be melancholy and are thus more prone to developing self-esteem issues. Individuals who have been exposed to trauma in childhood, struggled academically for long periods of time, and those with persistently negative thought patterns tend to have low self-esteem and may also have mental health conditions.

SELF-ESTEEM AND BRAIN FUNCTION

Neuroimaging is *"a clinical specialty concerned with producing images of the brain by noninvasive techniques (such as computed tomography and magnetic resonance imaging) or imaging of the brain by these techniques."* Merriam-Webster Online Dictionary.

In a report carried in the scientific journal *eLife*, researchers found that neuroimaging signals in the brain show different activity as self-esteem goes up or down. Such studies help researchers in the development of diagnostic tools and methods, which, in turn, aid therapists in making more efficient and accurate diagnoses. The therapist is able to assess the potential of psychiatric disorders in patients and to develop interventions to help alleviate mental health challenges.

In one such findings, the researchers reported that

"low self-esteem is a vulnerability factor for numerous psychiatric problems, including eating disorders, anxiety disorders and depression."

— DR. GEERT-JAN WILL AT LEIDEN UNIVERSITY AND MAX PLANCK UCL CENTER FOR COMPUTATIONAL PSYCHIATRY & AGING RESEARCH.

In the test, participants had their brains scanned with an MRI scanner. The subjects were a group of strangers put into two groups. One group was instructed to give positive feedback shown with a thumbs up, and the other group was asked to favor negative feedback shown with a thumbs down.

Participants quickly learned to anticipate positive feedback from the groups offering positive feedback and braced for negative feedback from the groups that offered negative feedback. They would then receive negative feedback from the group where they anticipated positive feedback, after which they would be asked to say how that made them feel.

When an individual anticipated positive feedback but received negative feedback, their self-esteem dipped. The findings showed that people will take negative feedback badly when they expect positive feedback and this would impact their sense of self.

The brain scans from when the individual was manifesting lower self-esteem showed a shift in brain function. The brain activity fluctuated more in the insula and prefrontal cortex areas of the brain. Such fluctuations would also indicate the individuals more likely to suffer from mental health problems such as anxiety and depression. People with such brain fluctuations were more susceptible to mental health issues when they encountered challenges.

More work on people with low self-esteem continues to help identify social factors that enhance vulnerabilities toward mental health problems including anxiety, depression, suicidal thoughts, and other tendencies to self-harm.

SIGNS OF LOW SELF-ESTEEM

As you recognize by now, low self-esteem is a problem that affects your efficacy in life and in the things that are important to you. In this section, we will look at the signs of low self-esteem.

On a scale of either/or, where are you on the self-esteem scale? The self-esteem scale needs to be considered with sobriety as the idea of high self-esteem is erroneous. Most people who exhibit having high self-esteem are usually masking very low self-esteem.

For this book, we will adopt healthy and unhealthy self-esteem at each end of the scale with an improving self-esteem at the half-way mark. Therefore the scale will have three notches, namely:

1. Unhealthy self-esteem.
2. Improving self-esteem.
3. Healthy self-esteem.

Your sense of self when you are feeling positive and vibrant means you are confident about your abilities and competencies.

To begin your self-evaluation, identify if you have factors that may contribute to a broken-down sense of self. You will find a detailed section on the causes of low self-esteem in a later chapter. Additionally, beware of issues or circumstances that you have faced recently, or for some time in your life that have wounded your view of your worthiness, your abilities, and your competencies. A healthy self-esteem will fluctuate when situations have pummeled you to the ground. Examples include:

- The breakdown of a marriage or any other important relationship. Getting fired from a job you loved would fall in this category.
- Persistent inability to achieve important life goals. Whereas the inability initially stemmed from low self-esteem, the failure only makes your self-esteem worse.
- An economic slump that makes it difficult and sometimes impossible to easily meet your obligations, especially toward dependents in your care. This may be precipitated by the loss of a job.
- Any event that affects your physical abilities significantly. This could be disease, an accident, or just wear and tear as you age.

In some cases and because low self-esteem may be subtle, you may fail to recognize that you have manifestations of low self-esteem. It is also highly possible to believe you do not have a problem in a particular area. The value of this list, therefore, is to enhance self-awareness.

1. Negative Inner Monologue

How do you speak to yourself? If you predominantly focus on your flaws and diminish your strengths, that is a problem. Your inner dialogue is a constant companion. Having that companion as a constantly negative voice is emotionally draining. Listen keenly to what you have to say of yourself to yourself.

2. Self-Blame

When things go wrong, are you quick to blame something you did? Is it true that you are to blame, or do you prefer to ascribe wrongdoing to yourself in an effort to make others feel better? This comes from situations at home where you had to cover for the dysfunction in parents or guardians.

3. "The Sky is Falling" Syndrome

Have you met people who are always anticipating the worst? Is that you? When you make a decision, do you constantly second guess yourself? Do you tell yourself how that decision was probably the wrong decision? Do you cast doubt on your own choices because you think that things will definitely go wrong? This type of thinking is coupled with the internal monologue convincing you that you have made a mistake.

4. Always Being the Good One

Trying to please people, particularly at your own expense, comes close on the heels of doubting your decisions and choices. The individual will defer their choice to that of others. Usually, it is masked as seeking to please others. Unfortunately, the effort to please others is made at the expense of your own joy and satisfaction.

Additionally, they will go to great lengths to make sure everyone is happy. Many family *"doormats,"* the one manipulative family members use to clean all their hurts and messes, are people pleasers. They bend over backward to take away everyone's pain. Where that could be a good characteristic in its place, the problem arises when they constantly do it and to their own detriment.

5. Inability to Receive Commendation

Positive feedback is critical in helping one to move forward with the things they do well. Positive feedback is also an important element in the mentor-mentee and teacher-student relationships. Unfortunately, the mind of the individual with low self-esteem is hardwired to say, *I am not good enough.* When they receive commendation, they instantly label it as false.

How do you respond to compliments? How does a positive remark make you feel? If you have done something well and someone makes a comment about it, what do you tell yourself? In some cases, commendation will lead the individual to self-sabotage on the next task because they tell themselves they are being taken for a ride. Their beliefs about their abilities conflict with the positive feedback.

6. Over Sensitivity to Feedback

Not all feedback is positive. Everyone encounters correction or suggestions for improvement in the relationships between the recipient and with mentors, teachers, or leaders. The individual with low self-esteem will not take such feedback for its merit. They will turn it around in their minds, contort it, and eventually turn it into a point of self-hurt. The individual already believes they are not good enough. Any additional information that seeks to help them reach a higher level of success is not seen for what it is, but as a confirmation that they are not good enough.

The individual with low self-esteem does not hear things said as they are said. They hear what is said from the existing bias that they are the problem. Their internal monologue will distort what is said and how it is said. That is not to say that any time someone is hurt by feedback, they have low self-esteem. The way to assess is to listen to the additional ways you interpret what was said. If you add negativity to the feedback, then the negativity was already hounding you from within.

7. Recurrent Self-Sabotage

Here, an individual who gets positive feedback will unconsciously work hard to do their worst on the next task to confirm to themselves that they are not what the other person saw. Self-sabotage is driven by the inner dialogue that says, *"You never get anything right, and you are not good enough."*

Self-sabotage also manifests as an uncanny ability to say the wrong things at the wrong time or create obstacles where there were none. At work, it manifests as making careless mistakes. Since the mind is wired to believe in an inability to excel, individuals with low self-esteem will make unnecessary mistakes because their brain will miss them.

When they come upon an opportunity, the individual with low self-esteem will miss the date only to discover it when it is too late. They will miss the fine print on an announcement and go right ahead to do the very thing the announcement said not to do. This is a reverse way in which the brain ensures that the inner dialogue of *"I never get anything right"* becomes a reality. Internal narratives are self-fulfilling prophecies.

8. Comparing Self with the Most Negative Example

Individuals with low self-esteem are also deeply concerned with how others see them. They magnify every small problem they perceive in themselves, mostly because they believe it is a big thing. They have an unhealthy preoccupation with every small manifestation of a problem.

In this preoccupation, they tend to compare themselves with the lowest possible examples available. When such an example does not exist, they will diminish whatever is available to the lowest possible level. They will say things like, *"My outfit was bad, but did you see that monstrosity so and so was wearing?"* or, *"Yes, my car is not as new, but have you seen the tin can so and so drives?"*

9. Belief in Failure

Lack of self-esteem is also a belief in failure. Remember that most people start their low self-esteem journey in childhood. That means they learned from very early that life does not work the way people imagine it should. If other children are speaking about cooperative parents at home, this child has uncooperative parents who barely speak to each other. They know from their own observation that family does not work the way everyone else says it does.

The adult with low self-esteem has so many factors that are out of alignment that they constantly remind themselves that their reality is the right one. Unfortunately, the reality they hold is not always the most common reality. There are many more opportunities for success than there are opportunities for failure. The inner dialogue is where success or failure dwell.

10. Too Fluid in Their Boundaries

The child growing in a healthy environment knows their limits. They know what they can say, what they can do, and what others can say or do to them. Not so the child who grows up in a dysfunctional environment. The effect is that as an adult, the individual, usually one with low self-esteem, will not have their boundaries in place.

They cannot say *"yes"* to the things they want and are equally unable to say *"no"* to the things they do not want. They will accept things they do not want because they are afraid of being seen as a bad person.

They are also terrified of losing favor with others. Remember, some of them have lived with manipulative individuals. Manipulative people will threaten children, for example, with loss of favors if they do not do what they are told to do, even when the demand hurts the child.

As the individual grows up, they lose the sense of self-preservation and always defer to pleasing others. Their space, property, time, and in some cases even their physical bodies are abused because they cannot say *"no"* or *"yes"* where it applied.

In relationships, individuals with low self-esteem have a problem with stating their needs in ways that enable their partner to meet said needs. They may exhibit two extremes. They will blame the partner for not knowing they needed something rather than express the need. Alternatively, they will ask for a completely different thing, hoping that the partner will somehow understand the unspoken need they are indirectly reaching for. This inability to express themselves constructively is deeply harmful to their relationships.

EXTREME CASES OF LOW SELF-ESTEEM

When low self-esteem has ravaged the individual and goes on unchecked, it starts to degenerate into mental health challenges and antisocial behavior.

Extremely low self-esteem is at the back of many severe personality disorders. The overpowering narcissist who borders on being cruel, or is in fact, cruel, is often a person with a deeply low sense of self. They want to cause others harm so they feel as much or more pain than they feel. They derive a sense of reassurance that they are indeed as bad as they think they are.

This downward spiral causes them to hate themselves more. Since they do not have a healthy inner dialogue, they will blame others for their pain and thus cause more pain.

On the extreme end, an individual who poses as having very high self-esteem also has extremely low self-esteem.

Ordinarily, listening to how someone speaks about themselves will tell you a lot about how they think about themselves. However, you may encounter a person who is always boasting about one thing or another. It is a façade intended to camouflage the sense of worthlessness that they could be feeling within.

In truth, they depend on other people's opinion of them to feel worthy. They therefore go out of their way to give an impression of being the best. In reality, they are masking a poor sense of self.

Given these extremes, you can see how low self-esteem may not always be easy to identify. Yet the impact on the individual remains emotionally draining.

1. Withdrawing From Social Interaction

An early sign of trouble is extreme discomfort and subsequent avoidance of social interaction. Self-isolation is the next stage from unchecked low self-esteem. The individual will decline invitations to social gatherings, parties, meeting up with friends, and will often find excuses – not reasons – to cancel prior arrangements at short notice.

They will avoid conversations that seek to draw them into the group. What is happening is their inner dialogue is on overdrive and running such a strong argument against everything that is happening in the group. They will tell themselves how they are not pretty, they are not dressed right, they do not know how to talk to others, and on and on it will go.

An individual who has slipped into self-isolation will rarely volunteer to speak honestly about what is going on within them. Remember, their world has been so severely distorted that they do not know what to believe in and what to doubt. So even speaking about their experience feels fraudulent because their views are so far removed from what everyone else is saying.

This is the time to seek out professional help. It is much better to sound unsettled to a therapist than to keep the voices and negative self-talk bottled up within. First, the therapist will not judge; secondly, they are qualified to help.

2. Gravitating Towards Hostility

On the same self-isolation continuum, the individual who has shifted from low self-esteem to severe low self-esteem will behave like a wounded animal because they are hurting very deeply. They respond to regular conversation with aggression. The idea is to get people away from them, and the self-isolation only plunges them deeper into hurt and despair. As said earlier, if you identify your most frequent response is to feel angry or affronted, it is time to seek therapy. Rarely do people go out of their way to actively attack. Thus if you are feeling attacked, you have an inner dialogue that is not supporting you. It is good to find help.

LOW SELF-ESTEEM CAUSES PHYSICAL PROBLEMS

The findings of many therapists and researchers point to the downward spiral of low self-esteem into health issues with physical symptoms. Eating disorders such as anorexia and bulimia go hand in hand with a low sense of self.

Emotional disorders, including anxiety, panic attacks, and depression, go hand in hand with low self-esteem. Substance abuse, suicide ideation, and deviant behavior such as getting into petty crime-gangs are also common in young people with low self-esteem. Risky behavior, including some already mentioned, but particularly those that expose the individual to life-threatening health problems often have direct correlation with low self-esteem.

The worst part about the individual deteriorating into deeply unhealthy levels of low self-esteem is they are often unable to find the help they so deeply need. If they become parents, then they trigger a cycle of dysfunction in homes leading to more children with low self-esteem.

Chapter Summary

In this chapter, we have looked at the signs of low self-esteem. We have touched on how low self-esteem develops. Most importantly, we have looked at areas of concern and how they relate to the degeneration into self-harm. This makes self-esteem issues an important conversation in saving lives.

In the next chapter, we will take a deeper look at the causes of low self-esteem. Thereafter, we will provide a self-evaluation section that will anchor the rest of this workbook in helping you develop your best and most practical self-therapy or professional help to others.

4

CAUSES OF LOW SELF-ESTEEM

In this chapter, we will look at the causes of low self-esteem with particular attention on childhood. We will then discuss the impact of abuse on self-esteem. Toward the end of the chapter, we will look at the impact of emotional neglect on the development of self-esteem.

Although there are many causes of low self-esteem, many or most of them will start to plague the individual in their developmental years as a child. In some people, the extreme effects of low self-esteem mentioned in the previous chapter will show up in their teens but reach a peak in adulthood.

It is, however, important to note that even those challenges that show up in adulthood often stem from childhood. This makes childhood the most significant season of an individual's life in the development of a healthy sense of self.

THE IMPACT OF DYSFUNCTIONAL HOMES

"Dysfunctional home" is a generic term that covers many aspects of the family that are not working. A child growing up in a dysfunctional home will almost always have effects leftover, which will show up in their definition of self. The toxicity of the environment, much like eating toxic food, impedes the development of the physical body and disrupts the development of a healthy sense of self.

The list below is another type of self-evaluation. You may recognize the circumstances of the home you grew up in if they are mentioned. Important note: the term "*parents*" also includes homes with one parent and families with a guardian or guardians. Here is a quick list of factors that may be present in a dysfunctional home...

- Parents who are constantly angry either at each other or at children.
- Homes where parents shout to express their emotions.

- Controlling behavior such as parents telling one another fabricated stories to elicit a specific response. Children are very aware of these types of adult games.
- Parents do not listen to children. They also do not listen to each other.
- Children of parents with a low sense of self.
- Emotionally repressed parents. That is, parents who never show any emotion, positive or negative.
- Highly critical parents and those that shame children. This is particularly harmful if the shame targets the child's legitimate emotional expressions.
- Parents who actively mock a child's physical abilities, appearance, or skills. In this category are also children of sexual misalignment and thus different sexual orientation.
- Homes with physical abuse of one parent to another or from parents to children.
- Children subjected to emotional abuse. Emotional abuse happens when there is constant haranguing of children, coupled with telling them hurtful statements such as they are useless and worthless.

- Homes where the parents have poor relationship skills and the children are privy to the dysfunction in the relationship.
- Uncooperative parents who may either not cooperate with each other, or may fail to cooperate with children when they could have.
- Parents who have no clear boundaries and who keep shifting the rules.
- Parents who do not offer a clear yes or no during similar or the same situations, but may change the answer when it suits them.
- Indifference. Parents who simply ignore children and expect them to keep to their own devices.
- Unsafe homes. The lack of safety could be within the home and in some cases, within the neighborhood. Children brought up in abject poverty are more likely to be affected by the effects of lack than those in fairly comfortable circumstances.

THE IMPACT OF DYSFUNCTION ON THE CHILD

A child growing in a home with one or more of these circumstances learns that they cannot trust. They lose their place in society as they do not have the stability that ordinarily would come from parents showing them the way.

Such children become preoccupied with the conversations they build within. Their inner conversations become more severe as the child does not have a healthy way of expressing them to the adults that could have provided a safe place for such self-expression.

Additionally, children who grow up in dysfunctional homes learn to hide their fear and feelings of inadequacy. They learn that being vulnerable is an opening for whatever form of dysfunction or abuse they are subjected to.

They learn to repress their emotions, their thoughts, their interests, and try as much as possible to blend in. This blending-in develops into the child, adolescent, and eventually, the adult having a learned inability to trust their own judgment and abilities. Any effort to draw them out may result in the indi-

vidual lashing out as they feel threatened by attention. They can even become aggressive, depending
on the depth of insecurity they feel.

Emotional repression lays a foundation for social
challenges such as anxiety or a deep sense of insecurity. Even in a room full of loving people, an individual growing up in a dysfunctional environment
will feel ignored or abandoned. When they do something well or correctly, they are still more likely to
blame themselves if anything goes wrong, even if
they had nothing to do with the error.

Friends of individuals who have grown up in a
dysfunctional environment soon learn that inter-
acting with the individual is like walking on
eggshells. The one with a low sense of self becomes
more withdrawn as they do not understand the way
to healthy socializations and building friendships. In
the extreme, they develop unhealthy co-dependency
on others. They seek validation at every turn as they
do not have the inner mettle to validate their own
decision-making process.

Overall, the inner dialogue of the individual says, "*I
am not good enough.*" They have a deep-seated sense
of shame rather than a sense of worthiness. They
are afraid to meet themselves, because if they find

that what they have within cannot hold them together, they are terrified that they will completely fall apart.

They already mistrust themselves in general, so any threat to their tenuous hold on life sends a deep terror through them. This fear of self may evolve to self-hate if the individual does not find a way to better self-expression. They develop an inner monologue that says:

- *I am unlovable.*
- *I never get it right.*
- *I am worthless.*
- *I can never measure up to others.*
- *Everyone is always better than I am.*
- *I do not deserve good things.*
- *I will never succeed at anything.*

The negative self-evaluations grow more antagonistic and hostile toward self as they go through each life experience. Therefore, it is particularly important that this individual learns to speak better to themselves. If unchecked, such highly negative inner conversations will lead to depression. Some individuals may even develop a suicide ideation conversation within. So, it is best if the individual learns ways to overcome the fear of self and of others.

ABUSE AND HOW IT AFFECTS SELF-ESTEEM

The online encyclopedia, Wikipedia, defines abuse as

"...physical, sexual, and/or psychological maltreatment or neglect of a child or children, especially by a parent or a caregiver. Child abuse may include any act or failure to act by a parent or a caregiver that results in actual or potential harm to a child and can occur in a child's home, or in the organizations, schools, or communities the child interacts with."

— THE ONLINE ENCYCLOPEDIA

The Mayo Clinic Guide to Raising a Healthy Child defines sexual abuse, emotional abuse, and neglect as follows:

- **Sexual abuse** is *"any sexual activity with a child. This can involve sexual contact, such as intentional sexual touching, oral-genital contact or intercourse. This can also involve noncontact sexual abuse of a child, such as exposing a child to sexual activity or pornography; observing or filming a child in a sexual manner; sexual harassment of a child; or prostitution of a child, including sex trafficking."*

- **Emotional abuse** means *"injuring a child's self-esteem or emotional well-being. It includes verbal and emotional assault — such as continually belittling or berating a child — as well as isolating, ignoring or rejecting a child."*

- While **neglect** refers to *"failure to provide adequate food, clothing, shelter, clean living conditions, affection, supervision, education, or dental or medical care."*

Abuse in any of its forms as defined above, has a negative impact on the child. To start with, all children will make some effort to stop the abuse, but without success. This in itself gives them a sense of defeat. If the abuse is repeated and goes on over a long period, the sense of defeat can be crippling. Other feelings that the child will internalize include shame and self-disgust. In some cases, the child will turn the hate toward themselves, arguing that if they had been different in some way, the abuser would not have had incentive to abuse them.

These feelings impact the development of the internal dialogue the individual will maintain within. Most sexual abuse is coupled with emotional and verbal abuse. The abuser plants the seeds of self-doubt and self-loathing in the victim's mind. The victim develops a thought process in a loop that evolves into psychological abuse initiated by the abuser and carried on in the victim's mind, making themselves their deepest enemy. Their inner voice may take on the voice of the abuser, and any time they hear the words repeated in their minds, they are a replay of the abuse.

In many cases, the voice of the emotional and psychological abuse takes on the individual's own voice, but the words remain those of the abuser. If, for instance, a parent would shame a child's physical appearance, the child may repeat the same abuse to themselves, but in their own voice.

It is this unintended self-abuse that triggers the ideation toward self-harm. The individual is trying to get away from the violent inner monologue in their head. Abuse in all its forms is the most violent form of destruction on self-esteem. The individual feels perpetually defeated and has a violent and abusive internal dialogue.

Many abusive partners may take to telling their spouse hurtful things, may be sexually abusive, or possibly emotionally abusive. If the victim of abuse in such a relationship has a history of abuse in their childhood, then the voices in their head compound to tear down their sense of self to shreds.

It may turn out to be more difficult for a childhood victim of abuse to clear the abuse pattern than for an individual who is in an abusive relationship as an adult. Usually, however, few people will end up in an abusive relationship and prolong it if their self-esteem is healthy. Many people who end up in abusive relationships already have a self-esteem problem, often one that is rooted in childhood.

Emotional abuse, specifically, may start in adulthood and in adults who have no previous history of abuse, but do have a self-esteem problem. Either party may start out with a desire to control or manipulate the other party. If they have low self-esteem, they feel inadequate and believe the only way their partner can cooperate is if they tear them down so that they cannot offer any resistance to the abuser's will.

Over time and in such verbally violent relationships, the abused party will start to believe what they are told. The result is a reduced sense of self and again, if they do not break away from the abuse or get help, the low self-esteem may start to produce physical manifestations as discussed earlier.

Adults who have had a brush with events that trigger a low sense of self may turn out to be the abuser. They lash out at the other partner they feel did not get as bad a deal as they did. The goal of the abuse is to make the other party feel as bad about themselves as they feel. They want to trigger feelings of guilt, fear, hopelessness, impotence, and helplessness in the other party.

EFFECTS OF EMOTIONAL NEGLECT

According to the Encyclopedia of Human Behavior, Volume 2, emotional neglect is

---

"a relationship pattern in which an individual's affectional needs are consistently disregarded, ignored, invalidated, or unappreciated by a significant other."

— ENCYCLOPEDIA OF HUMAN
BEHAVIOR, VOLUME 2

People with multiple personality challenges may be unable to be effective parents to their children. Emotional development is a crucial stage in the optimum developmental stages in the child. Children learn how to feel about their world through interaction with their parents. If this interaction is not present, then the child's emotional development needs are stunted.

It is through parents or caregivers that a child learns healthy and unhealthy attachments to others. If a parent is inattentive, distracted, or generally unavailable to the child, then the child does not get necessary feedback to learn how to process their emotions.

Neglect may also take the form of a complete lack of connection with the child. This manifests when a parent is unable to express their emotional responses in ways that a child will understand. Children will go through similar emotional responses as parents. These include fear, joy, happiness, surprise, contentment, etc. A child who receives nurture will learn to process these emotions as they grow older based on what they see in their parents.

In families that do not express their emotions and where they offer inadequate nurture, particularly from the primary caregiver or the mother of the child, there is learned repression of emotions or an inability to express one's emotions well. The inability to express emotions may arise when the parent feels the child needs too much attention. Emotional neglect may also arise if a parent is mostly fatigued. They may lack the energy to be present to offer love and emotional attention to the child.

If a child is frustrated or angry, for instance, a parent can help them process these feelings by being present and talking the child through the feelings. In younger children, the talking may be a soothing voice, but as they grow older, it is giving them ways to feel better from a negative emotion or help them enjoy a positive emotion. If the parent is not able to be present, they may ignore and treat what the child is expressing as unimportant. In this way the child learns that their emotional responses are irrelevant, unimportant, or outrightly shameful.

Holding them, showing love and affection, open conversations, and support in difficult times are all ways that the caregiver or parents of the child teach them to manage their emotions. The parent may be unable to express their emotions because they too come from a background where repressed emotions were the norm. They may have grown into unfulfilling relationships as adults because they could not express their emotions and emotional needs. Such individuals will not be able to give emotional attention to the child.

The child from emotionally repressed backgrounds learns to deal with their emotions in the best way they know how. They may develop healthy or unhealthy ways to deal with their emotions. If they learn unhealthy ways, this will affect their sense of self. They will tell themselves that their emotions are inappropriate and unnecessary. They are afraid to express all emotions, whether positive or negative. They may also develop an unhealthy attachment to their emotions so that whatever they feel is amplified to the extreme.

Ignored children may develop behavioral challenges. Aggression, hyperactivity, and hurtful or inappropriate language are all ways in which a child may act out against emotional neglect. They are looking for ways to get attention, but go about it the wrong way, because no one taught them the right way. These behaviors add to a low sense of self and in time may develop into antisocial behavior such as running away from home or joining groups that support indiscipline.

They may develop emotional disorders such as anxiety and panic attacks. Some may even develop eating disorders or other behaviors toward self-harm. As they continue to develop, they will be unable to form healthy relationships with others, gravitate toward unhealthy attachments to others, and generally not know how to manage their emotions within the context of relationships.

For example, they may accuse their partner of being unloving and inattentive, but they may be the ones who are not able to express those emotions. In some instances, they may not know how to rightly interpret those emotions when expressed by another.

Intimacy is difficult for people who have grown in an emotionally neglectful environment. They do not know how to express vulnerability and may find it shameful or even threatening.

Children without sufficient nurturing and emotional attention will simply not thrive and often exhibit delayed developmental milestones. Such children are unable to enjoy the usual creativity and joy of life present in most children. They become shy and reserved.

An inability to adequately express self will plague the individual with an emotionally neglected background. Unlike people who have developed their emotional abilities in a healthy manner, this individual feels awful and may be unable to congratulate themselves when things are going well. They feel inadequate most of the time and these feelings contribute to a low self-esteem.

Practical Self-Evaluation

We have gone through the development and manifestations of low self-esteem. The self-evaluation below will give you a basis to understand your self-esteem. It will also help you to map how you got to this level of self-esteem. It will help you look at your developmental stages and see how some events may have contributed to where you are in your sense of self today.

It is mapped to a series of negative assertions followed by a series of positive assertions. Use each to rate yourself, identifying if you feel that way most of the time or only some of the time. At the end of the exercise, rate yourself by checking which rating appears most often.

To evaluate yourself, use the following markers. On reading the assertion and after evaluating myself, this statement is true for me...

- Most of the time
- Rarely
- Never

Give yourself an overall score based on the answers you gave as follows:

- If you answer "most of the time" 7 times or more, you have an "unhealthy sense of self."
- If you answer is "rarely" 4 to 6 times, you have an "improving sense of self"
- If you answer "never" less than 7 times, you have a "healthy sense of self"

Positive Assertions

1. I feel that I am not enough.
2. I have no way of improving myself.
3. I feel valueless and unimportant.
4. I doubt my abilities and feel incompetent and fear taking risks.
5. I do not think I am a very good person. I dislike myself.
6. I prefer to agree with others to avoid drawing attention to myself.
7. If I need to make a decision, I doubt my ability to choose well and prefer to ask others for their opinion.
8. I distrust praise and will find a way to deflect it or counter it when it is spoken.

9. I do not know how to express my emotional needs and find it ridiculous to ask for what I need.
10. I dread starting new things because I am likely to get it wrong.
11. I put others first because I want them to like me.
12. I am afraid that if I say no or yes when I should, people will find me obnoxious and will not like me.
13. Most people can do things much better than I ever could.
14. In a room full of people, I will feel anxious, alone, and may even have a panic attack.
15. If I am corrected, I feel affronted and attacked. I hate being corrected and receiving feedback.

Now go through the following positive assertions. Once again rate yourself against the following parameters:

- Most of the time
- Rarely
- Never

Give yourself an overall score based on the answers you gave as follows:

- If you answer "most of the time" 7 times or more, you have a "healthy sense of self."
- If you answer is "rarely" 4 to 6 times, you have an "improving sense of self"
- If you answer "never" less than 7 times, you have an "unhealthy sense of self."

Positive Assertions

1. I know I am okay.
2. I know that I am valuable and that I matter in my world and to others.
3. Feel competent and confident in my skills, abilities, and general person.
4. I am a good person and I like myself.
5. It is easy for me to be honest and exhibit integrity in my relationships and work.
6. I enjoy and appreciate praise. It makes me feel great that I am doing things right.
7. Attention is a good thing. It says what I am doing has an impact.

8. I am confident in my ability at self-control, emotional control, and general control of myself.
9. Pursuing my goals makes me feel vibrant and alive as I am confident I have what it takes to accomplish them.
10. I respect myself and respect others too.
11. When others get a good break, I am happy for them and know that mine is on its way too.
12. The people around me are as they are. I do not feel the need to change them.
13. Relationships are fulfilling, thrilling, and give me new insights into the other person and into myself.
14. I am able to express myself and my boundaries clearly and assertively.
15. I am confident that I can build new relationships and friends in a room full of people.

In the next chapter, we will look at your inner critic.

5

THE INNER CRITIC

So far, we have detailed how inner dialogue, monologues, or self-talk works. You have seen the conversation that takes place within each individual in different manifestations of low self-esteem. If you completed the self-test in the last chapter, you should have a fairly good idea where your self-esteem lies on the scale. Additionally, as you have read causes, signs, and the impact of the home you grew up in on your self-esteem as an adult, you can see how your own issues play out.

We move into the next aspect of this conversation. So far, we have detailed the problem: low self-esteem. We now discuss the solutions to the problem and ways to improve your self-esteem.

In every area we have looked at where low self-esteem is evident, the inner voice shows up. In this chapter, we will dwell on the inner critic to offer ways to take charge in how you speak to yourself. The goal is to improve your inner conversations and make them more positive.

YOUR INNER DIALOGUE AS A PART OF WHO YOU ARE

Throughout this book, keep listening to how you speak to yourself. You will find that you have quite the chatter going on within you. As mentioned, some of your conversations may take the voice of a parent, others may be your voice, and others will be the voice of someone in your past who was mean to you. That is mostly true if you are rehashing the mean things said to you. In some people, the voice shifts at different times of their life, depending on the experiences they are going through.

This consistent voice that triggers feelings of being less than, is what we refer to as the inner critic. In most people, the tone and gender of that voice is consistent. For most of us, we have lived with this way of thinking and speaking to ourselves for so long that we believe it is who we are. It has become a part of our personality. If we were to defend the way we speak to ourselves, we would say,

"It is just the way I am."

If we accept that voice as who we are, then we do not care to change it. We have continuous self-inflicted pain. Additionally, whether we think this way or not, that voice is still a very personal part of who we are. As such, the work to change such an integral aspect of ourselves is difficult.

This is the reason why hearing how you speak to yourself is important, however, it is not a change that will somehow sort itself out. It has to be a deliberate and conscious change. Deliberate in that you have to **want** to change it. So how do you go about it?

SEPARATE THE VOICE FROM YOURSELF

The key is to decide that you are done with trash-talking yourself. It does not matter if the voice takes on several different personalities, you are done with them all. You want change. You are ready to change.

You will do whatever it is that you need to do to get a different life experience.

- **The first step is to consciously give your inner critic a new personality that is distinctly different from you.** Some experts suggest you use a cartoon character or a person you are not fond of. Consider making it something small and potentially harmless like a talking hamster. Remove the power of this voice by making it small and unreal. This also helps you to question or ignore what it says as you will see in the next steps.
- **Learn to listen to your inner dialogue consciously.** Not all the counsel that comes from your inner critic is worth keeping. Some of it is just empty chatter, some outright lies, especially if it is repeating words from an abuser, and a portion is just cruel criticism. Ask yourself questions like, *"Is that true?"*
- **Tune out the incessant nagging and replace it with clear questions** so that your mind can give you instructions to deal with a problem. *"How do I do this?"* is a good

question to pose to your new inner voice. Reach for counsel, guidance, and constructive feedback.

- **Make friends with your inner voice.** Yes, abusers and people who did not understand the development of a child or even people who lived in fear and spoke to you out of their fear have given you an inner voice that does not support you. However, the real you wish nothing but good and well-being for you. This is what happens as you start to ask for guidance. The real you, who is your friend and best champion, will start to show up more.

The real you will never put you down, and that is the most important thing you need to realize. When you feel a tinge of unease or anxiety, tune in to what is going on within you. If your inner voice has turned critical and harsh, that is *not* you. Tune in to the guidance and counsel. You will find you have a delightful ally in all your life efforts.

RECAPTURE YOUR POWER

Conscious listening will sometimes take you back to a past experience. You will find that what you consciously remember of the event and what your mind has stored may be two very different things.

Example: Say you had a mean teacher. In your mind, they were always trying to put you down. However, now that you start listening consciously you realize they were actually giving you feedback, but because you had a self-esteem problem, you heard it all wrong.

When that is your experience, work it backward until you can find the point at which you started doubting yourself. You will be surprised how far back the mind can go into your stored memories. The value of this exercise is to see your life from the eyes of the adult and to integrate the experiences. It will help you take the edge off difficult situations when you learn that you are now no longer a powerless victim.

THE CRITICAL INNER VOICE AND ABUSE

So far we have spoken of the critical inner voice of individuals who have low self-esteem but who are not necessarily working on themselves from trauma resulting from abuse. For the victim of abuse, their inner voice may be way crueler toward them and aggressive to others. The inner voice will still be an active and ongoing inner dialogue, but it will be more inclined to being violent and antisocial.

The victim of abuse has learned to cope by self-protecting against a hostile world. Their inner critic, therefore, serves to keep them safe. The method of safety will also incline the individual toward maladaptive behavior. This voice, just as the earlier one, will not be a friend and ally within. The inner monologue will be present to sustain a system of thoughts and attitudes that tend to be harmful to the individual.

The task of the victim of abuse will be to continuously evaluate life to sift out the experiences that support their wellbeing. They may find that their inner communication is inclined toward turning their heart and mind against society because that is where the pain and abuse came from. Left unchecked, the inner voice in some victims will affirm thoughts and attitudes that are limiting and lead them to both attacks against self as well as attacks against others.

What we are all reaching for is a point of inner harmony where what we think and what we say and do are all aligned to the one task of ensuring our wellbeing. So, although they will find that their inner dialogue splits their experience between who they are and the way the world appears, the ultimate goal for all is to gain inner self-support and affirmation of worthiness.

The pathway to self-support is similar as the one discussed above:

- Start by listening to yourself and identifying how inclined you are to negate the good in your life. Do you build up every experience to be harmful to you and thus you feel the need to protect yourself? Hearing how you speak to yourself will give you room to be objective about the influences within you.
- Give your inner voice a personality you can easily silence and even ignore. The power of the abuser, now that you are all grown up,

remains in your fear of them. Remove their ability or their influence over you by making them small and weak.

- Question the dialogue. Where are the thoughts leading you? Be objective. What is harmful? Admit that it is harmful.

- Restructure your mind resources to work with you toward problem-solving.

- Find a person who can help you work out the monologue in your mind. A therapist is professionally equipped to help in a non-judgmental way and to enable you to make tangible progress toward a more solution-based inner dialogue.

- The goal is to find the inner voice that is your friend. This voice will support you and give you delightful ideas on ways to overcome challenges and gradually develop a more fulfilling life experience.

TAKING AWAY POWER FROM HARMFUL THINKING

We have mentioned several times that it is important to learn to listen to your inner monologue. The question is, what are you listening for? What is harmful thinking and why is it so? Harmful thoughts will have three major characteristics.

1. They are familiar, spontaneous, and invasive.

They are there, popping into your mind seemingly from nowhere. You have grown used to such thoughts, and they even sound like you. You do not find a reason to question them because you already believe them. There is a belief for every situation, conversation, or interaction you have. They are always present and running a commentary about everything you are experiencing.

2. They are actually false.

The premise they present usually collapses on investigation. Their truthfulness does not hold up to the question, *"Is that true?"* Most of them are factually false. They are distortions your mind has developed over time.

3. They do not support your well-being or what is best for you.

They limit your potential. They question your ability. They undermine your skills and knowledge. They give you reasons why you are not good enough. They seek to bring you down and not to build up your confidence.

THE LANGUAGE OF HARMFUL INNER MONOLOGUES

Harmful inner monologues have specific language formats common to them. They present their case in a certain way and are easy to miss unless you are paying attention so that you quickly spot their language. Here is a list of some of the ways they show up.

1. Your inner dialogue paints a gloomy picture.

As mentioned, your inner dialogue will help you see the world. You see the world from the narration that you carry on within. Is that inner dialogue telling you everything is gloom and doom? If you are unable to shake off the deep negativity, it is beneficial to seek help from a professional with whom you can speak freely about what you feel.

2. Your thoughts blame you for emerging events.

"It's all my fault."

No! It is not *all* your fault!

There are very few things in life that are entirely up to one individual. Usually, there are small or large contributions from several people in most things. Remember the voice of the abuser or the critic who kept blaming you for things that had transpired? Do not do the same to yourself. You do not always have to blame something and you certainly should not blame yourself.

3. Thinking in superlatives such as, *"This always happens to me."*

Watch your internal language and pick out superlatives and generalizations.

- *I **always** do this.*
- *This **always** happens to me.*
- *I **never** get it right.*
- *I **never** know what to do.*
- ***No one** understands me.*
- *I **always** mess things up.*
- ***People** suck!*

Besides putting you into a mental cycle of self-fulfilling defeat, generalizations are untrue. It is a false statement. When you hear the superlative, even in speech, stop and ask yourself, *"Really?"* Thinking in superlatives and generalizations is defeatist. It is your way of not giving yourself a chance for any other option. It plunges you into self-sabotage.

4. Playing God About Events

Very close to an inner dialogue that runs on superlatives is making conclusions about things without any evidence to support your claim, not even to yourself. Give life a chance. This applies to how you read people. Do not jump to conclusions about what people are going to say or what they are thinking. Give people a chance. Examples include:

- *This is going to be very bad.*
- *This can never end well.*
- *This will not work out.*

5. Beliefs That Support the Worst Case Scenario

Let us say you were trying on a new outfit for an upcoming event. Then the button fell off and the seam tore as you were trying it on. In harmful thinking, you will concentrate on that one bit that did not go right and ignore all the other things that were positive and went according to plan. If your inner monologue is used to running riot, you will map out why that bit was symbolic and why it is a sign that the upcoming event shall be an absolute failure. That is not even mildly true. If the overall experience was positive, do not pick the one negative and make it the entire experience. That is defeatist.

6. Making All People Horrible

You have ten colleagues, but one is unpleasant. You then superimpose the unpleasant one on all the other nine and make *everyone* bad. Similarly, you discussed with a boss or mentor and they spoke for 30 minutes. At minute 24, they challenged a decision you made. You then ignore everything else said in that meeting for the next couple of weeks. You keep reminding yourself that the boss is totally unappreciative of your efforts. Do not sabotage your relationships with others by generalizing and making them the worst.

7. If I Am Feeling It, That Is the Truth

"If I am feeling afraid, then in fact the situation is a threat." As you work on your inner dialogue, you may also discover that you tend to feel unsettled as a reaction to previous insecurities. If you have a fear of crowds, you may feel uncertain in a crowd, not because they are threatening, but because you have

existing disquiet about crowds. Question your feelings.

8. Forcing an Outcome on Events

When your inner dialogue demands pre-knowledge of an outcome, you set yourself up for trouble because life doesn't always turn out as expected. Listen to your inner dialogue for "should" and question it.

- *This should be like this.*
- *You should do this.*
- *You should have done this.*
- *I should have known.*

9. Personality Evaluations Based on Superficial Factors

You can develop a whole list of such judgments of personality based on superficial factors. Examples include:

- *People of this race are like this…*
- *People of this political inclination are like this…*
- *This gender is like this…*
- *People who live in this part of town are like this…*
- *People of this faith are like this…*

There is no group of people that are one homogenous mass who all think and act the same. It is simply not possible; people are individuals, each one with a unique personality and character. Therefore, if you hear a summation of what you will expect from a person based on a superficial factor, demand to know from your inner dialogue whether there is evidence for that thought.

BECOME AWARE OF YOUR TRIGGERS

We have worked our way through childhood and to how you develop an interplay between your inner dialogue and your self-esteem. As you observe your personal growth and how you have arrived at where you are now, you will discover that certain situations make you more vulnerable than others. You will have triggers that activate insecurities and pull you into a downward spiral of self-doubt. Most triggers will be around the areas where you are most uncomfortable.

If you have a history of being a victim of body shaming, someone making a slight reference to something about your body will trigger a sense of uncertainty. Whether the comment is positive or negative, it will still raise your anxiety.

If you have a history where you have become sensitive about your abilities, you will feel anxious if your performance is in focus. Here are other situations that may evoke negative inner dialogue and cause you to feel inadequate.

- ***Challenges in Your Relationship:*** If you are having problems in your relationship, beware that this will increase your feelings of inadequacy. If you already doubt your ability to bond with others, this will be a bad time for you.
- ***Circumstances That Make You Feel Sad:*** Any situation that brings on the blues will not be a good time for you. Emotions can catapult into each other and trigger stronger feelings of anxiety, anger, guilt, or shame. These are also the times that will evoke a relapse if you are in therapy.
- ***When You Need to Try Something New:*** Maybe you want to get a new job, move into a new neighborhood, or anything else that demands more from you. This might trigger your sense of inadequacy; hence, it is the time to be most conscious of your inner dialogue.

- A ***Circumstance That Demands Your Best Result:*** When you need to put your best foot forward, make a presentation, meet people for the first time, or any other situation that demands high performance will make you feel vulnerable.

- ***Situations Where You Are Under Scrutiny:*** Situations that will turn all eyes on you will make you feel vulnerable and may trigger all your inner dialogue on how you will mess it all up in some way. Do not entertain such thoughts. Focus on being yourself, and you will ace it.

- ***Fatigue, Lack of Rest, or Sickness:*** Situations in which you are not at your best will trigger your insecurities. Keep telling your inner critic to take a chill pill in those times.

Practical View

1. Open a journal and start jotting down the things you say to yourself. If you can isolate specific phrases for specific emotional states, that would be even better. Later on, study the words you say to yourself and identify if they are representative of who you are.

2. Go through your list above and create a personality for your negative inner voice. Put thought into this. Let your personality feel right for you, but make sure they are small and non-threatening.

3. Give yourself a question that you will defer to when your negative critic starts the chatter. You can choose to ask, *"Is that true?"* Alternatively, come up with a question that feels right for you.

In the next chapter, you will learn about specific CBT Skills.

6

CBT SKILLS

In the last chapter, we touched on the inner critic and how your inner voice develops. By now, you should have a fairly good sample of the things you say to yourself. If you have not started developing your list, start now. It will help make this chapter and the remaining chapters beneficial to you personally.

We have mentioned skills to help you hear your inner dialogue. We have also discussed how you can learn to question the inner voice. Questioning your inner voice is an important skill as it helps your conscious self to sift through the distortions your brain may have stored as fact over the years. As you are an adult now, your experiences will help you to objectively look at life, compare with what your inner critic says, and identify how the inner critic's voice is working against your well-being.

Keep in mind that the negativity of the inner critic does not make you a bad person. The data or information you have gathered in the course of your life experiences stand separate from you. They are not you. They are data. Data and information can and should be changed if they are not working in your favor.

In this chapter, we will discuss specific CBT skills.

1. Cognitive Reframing

According to Seth J. Gillihan, PhD in his book, *Retrain Your Brain*, Cognitive Reframing is

---

"a technique used to shift your mindset so you're able to look at a situation, person, or relationship from a slightly different perspective."

— SETH J. GILLIHAN, PHD

Cognitive reframing is a skill you use for yourself to shift your own cognitions. If you are working with a therapist, particularly if your inner critic is intense and you need assistance working through negative thought patterns and learned distortions in your inner voice, the same skill is known as *"cognitive restructuring."*

To help you see how cognitive reframing works, take an example of an individual who is having a difficult time at work. This is the second time in the year that he or she was passed over for a promotion. They are distraught and their inner critic is giving them a disparaging inner monologue about it. *"You are not good enough,"* or, *"no one will ever appreciate you in this office,"* and other similar statements are running riot in their minds.

The individual may pose a question to themself, *"Can anything good come out of this situation?"*

The individual may remember their other family obligations that, in fact, make a promotion at that particular time a bad idea as the new responsibilities at work would take time away from the family. They may remember that indeed they had signed up for a short course and the promotion's demand on their time would overwhelm them. They may also recall that they prefer their current position and are focused on a different job offer that would pay more, while this promotion would be a distraction more than a benefit.

Cognitive reframing is the difference between looking outside through a crack and moving over to look at the same scene through the window. You see more and gain more from the experience you are in. A similar process would occur with a therapist in the cognitive restructuring process.

2. Behavioral Activation

In discussing behavioral activation as a therapy for depression, Christopher Martell, Ph.D., offers these insights into the approach.

"Behavioral Activation seeks to help people understand environmental sources of their depression, and seeks to target behaviors that might maintain or worsen the depression.

While committed behavior therapists continued to utilize this approach much more research was conducted on cognitive-behavioral treatment for depression, which incorporated behavioral activation but focused mainly on the typical distortions in thoughts and beliefs that are characteristic of depressed individuals."

— CHRISTOPHER MARTELL, PH.D.

The goal of behavioral activation is to restore interest in activities that used to give the individual pleasure before they started slipping into depression. Other interventions in the therapy include *"activity monitoring"* to find a correlation between activities, sleep routines, and diet, which are all factors that could compound and aggravate the desire for avoidance and escape.

One of the effects of low self-esteem is the tendency to avoid both old and familiar activities as well as new activities. In behavioral activation therapy, either alone or with a therapist, the goal is to regain a sense of self that says, *"I am capable."* The individual develops better internal dialogue. They find better ways to cope with challenging situations and do not paint worst-case scenarios as soon as they are met with a slight obstacle.

3. Training in Assertiveness

With collapsed or weak boundaries and with low self-esteem, individuals generally have a harder time stating what they want. This can extend to both saying *"no"* and saying *"yes."* Learning to be assertive is a skill that everyone needs as it is beneficial in growing a career and for developing healthy relationships. Assertiveness will also serve you well as you become a happier person.

Lack of assertiveness also hinders the individual's ability to achieve their goals. For instance, a person who knows they need to take an extra study to improve their career may be unable to ask for a schedule that supports that goal.

In a relationship, one party may be unable to say that they do not like to participate in certain activities. Additionally, the inability to assert oneself means the individual with low self-esteem is unable to negotiate and compromise for a win-win. They are unable to speak out so that their relationships are fulfilling to them.

Around family and friends, an individual who is unable to be assertive will fail to let people know time and again when a request is inconvenient. As a behavioral therapy skill, assertiveness helps the individual to restore their sense of self and formulate their boundaries in fulfilling ways.

If an individual has a background of abuse, they may have learned to be timid to stay safe. They may have learned not to question authority even when said authority hurts them, because they were the weaker person in the relationship. They may have learned to hurt silently because that was the best self-preservation they had at the time.

These coping and behavioral skills transcend the abusive relationship and become a learned way of behavior that leaves the individual feeling unappreciated time and again. They feel that people take undue advantage of them, which leads to deeper feelings of worthlessness. Whether it is in relationships with friends and neighbors, at work, with family, or in specific careers such as sales, assertiveness enables the individual to carve out a place for themselves.

4. Problem-Solving

Growing children have developmental milestones where they progressively learn new skills that enable them to be more self-sufficient. They become more self-confident as they grow because they can handle certain skills. The child starts by not knowing which shoe goes on what foot. The day they get the shoe matrix right, they never struggle with putting on their shoes again.

The same is true of speech, dressing, and many aspects of self-care and grooming. However, setbacks such as an accident, a health problem, or even aging can trigger the loss of certain self-care skills that one had once mastered.

An athlete may lose a limb in an accident that makes them not only incapable of competing thereafter, but they may even be confined to using a walking aid. Accidents also lead to such clinical challenges as loss of memory. The accident victim may find that they need to re-learn details that once came to them easily. Others may find that they have to re-learn how to learn.

All such setbacks can have a severe impact on self-esteem, leading to recurrent feelings of worthless-ness. Where the individual was once sure of their abilities, now they are not.

Problem-solving in this context is training the indi-vidual to develop new methods of doing what they once knew but they may not do to the same level of efficiency anymore. The goal of problem-solving is to help the individual find new ways to be self-sufficient in view of the losses they have encountered.

Either on their own or with the help of a therapist, the goal of problem-solving skills is to help the individual objectively identify the problem. They then look at what resources they have available to them. Finally, the problem solving skill gives them new reference points to find solutions that support their well-being. If they need to develop proactive solutions to the setbacks, then the problem-solving skills give them a frame of reference to think through their options.

5. Social Skills Training

In explaining the use of Social Skills Training (SST) as an intervention in various behavioral disorders, Marsha M. Linehan, PhD says,

---

"Skills are designed to treat emotional dysregulation and its maladaptive consequences.

*...It is important to integrate positives and nega-
tives as life moves along. Without this integration,
there can be no real recovery."*

— MARSHA M. LINEHAN, PHD

Social skills training is used to enhance therapy for people with anxiety disorders, mood disorders, personality disorders, mental disorders, developmental disabilities, and other diagnoses.

There is a direct correlation between a drop in proficiency in social skills and the drop in self-confidence. What are social skills? Here is a list of fifteen skills. With a sense of defeat in just five or more of these, the individual starts to feel incompetent in human interactions.

1. Apologize without feeling shame.
2. Assert self without doubting oneself.
3. Good control of body language and self-expression.
4. Being able to collaborate with others.
5. Ability to hold your own in difficult conversations.

6. Being able to read your emotions and express them constructively.
7. Ability to empathize with others.
8. Knowledge of etiquette and the right things to do in particular circumstances.
9. Finding ways to forgive others and self.
10. How to build and keep friendships.
11. How to enjoy a good laugh and to have a sense of humor.
12. How to express self competently using words and language.
13. How to stick to a goal or task until you get desired results.
14. Ability to speak to others politely.
15. How to build meaningful relationships.

When an individual cannot gain competency in social skills that most people take for granted, they feel less competent in almost all other areas. This affects their sense of self and decreases their desire to interact with others. Self-isolation is a trigger for deeper emotional problems and a precursor to depression.

You can choose to enhance any social skill in a self-taught program. Most social skills have a course available online or in a book at the library or a book-store near you.

Alternatively, you can join other people to develop a particular skill. Learning with others has multiple benefits. It allows you to interact with others in a targeted interest. That in itself makes it easier to build friendships and launch conversations with others. Sharing a self-improvement program with like-minded people may help one to feel less incompetent as you are all learners.

Therapists also assist people in developing social skills. The more competent the individual feels and becomes, the more courage and confidence they gain. This is a great boost to their sense of self and boosts their self-esteem.

We will make reference to the above skills as we continue in the rest of the book with examples and ideas on ways to use each skill in context. Except for Social Skills Training, which works best with a coach or a professional therapist, you can develop a self-therapy model to use on yourself in all the other CBT skills. Although the individual in SST will often require assistance from a therapist, the individual will still be called upon to carry out the practice of the skills on their own.

DEVELOPING YOUR SELF-IMAGE

How do you view yourself?

Alongside your sense of self, there is how you view yourself in relation to others and to the world in general. This is your self-image.

In his bestselling classic, *Psycho-Cybernetics*, Maxwell Maltz, plastic surgeon and author, defines self-image as,

---

"The subconscious framework, of how we see life and ourselves. Everyone has one and most of us are not even aware of it, and that's a problem. It means we may have powerful beliefs about ourselves and the world that we can't challenge or change because we're not even aware of them."

— MAXWELL MALTZ, PLASTIC
SURGEON AND AUTHOR

We each develop our self-image through early childhood and a piece of how you see yourself is added to your overall view of self with every win or loss. The way guardians or caregivers spoke to us also contributed to the way we eventually view ourselves and our worth.

A child who develops in a home where they are constantly told how ugly they are, as an example, will have a challenge with believing they are beautiful later in life. This kind of false internal programming by those around us does not consider the factual status. Many beautiful people feel ugly and believe they are ugly because they received that assertion repeatedly in their past.

Poor self-image in caregivers also translates to a low self-image in the children. Dysfunction in adults who have children in their care may evolve to the same kind of dysfunction in the child to a greater or lesser degree. A woman who had body issues may pass on the anxiety to her child, especially a daughter. The man who believes he is worthless may turn against his child and cause severe harm to the child's self-image, causing the child to also believe they are worthless.

Self-image can be positive or negative. A positive self-image helps the individual to appreciate their strengths. Individuals with a healthy self-image will also pay close attention to their grooming and self-care. A poor self-image sees more of one's weaknesses, making them clumsy and incompetent even in situations where they would be exceptionally competent.

Physical appearance plays a big role in the way many people develop their self-image. This, in part, is an effect of digital and audio visual media. There is a lot of emphasis on looking a certain way in most mass productions, in print, and on social media. We grow up with a standard of what is an attractive look and tend to evaluate ourselves against this unconscious standard.

A positive self-image enhances our appreciation of ourselves and does not impede on our interactions with others and with the world. It also gives the basis upon which we grow our mental, social, and spiritual selves. We are more willing to add to our academic skills. We are comfortable in new and challenging social situations. We also feel that our place on the earth is secure, making it easier to follow a positive spiritual pathway.

DEVELOP YOUR SELF-IMAGE CONSCIOUSLY

As in all aspects of self-assessment, we do not develop self-image once and have it as a fixed marker for life. Some changes happen along the way that may affect how we see ourselves in that season.

Puberty in most children, and especially in girls, also gives rise to body-image anxiety. According to a piece carried in the Guardian and quoted from the 2014 British Social Attitudes survey, *"Only 63% of women aged 18-34 and 57% of women aged 35-49 are satisfied with their appearance."* The changes of the body in this season, coupled with the standards of what is an attractive body, can give young girls a lot of anxiety about how they look.

A change in economic circumstances may trigger a season of a poor self-image. The individual may not have the resources to continue with routine grooming. Their clothes may be older than they are comfortable with. They may be forced to drive a vehicle of a lesser quality than the one they would prefer. They may end up living in an area that was not of their choice.

A change in economics affects most adults more than many other things. They feel inadequate and the negative self-talk starts to show up in the way they carry themselves and their relationships, shifting the place they give to themselves in the world to a lower one.

It is possible to develop a confident self-image. Here are a few steps to follow:

1. Develop your own standard of attractiveness.

Although you might be tempted to use the measuring line placed on society by mass media, social media, and other publications, you can develop your own list of best attributes. Base your list on what you like and what you find attractive in others.

Couple this with your own dress sense. Some fashion styles will not work well on you, and others will be flattering. Go with the flattering styles. When do you feel most confident about yourself? What kind of clothes are you wearing when you feel confident? Build your wardrobe around that dress sense.

Do not be tempted to say attractiveness is blonde hair if you have black hair or five feet tall if you are six feet tall. Do not attribute attractiveness to a factor you cannot change about yourself. Make what you have look good because it is.

If you have an attribute that you are not too sure about, look for models that you consider good-looking who have a similar attribute. Start to consciously look around you to find the attributes you admire and see how great they look on others.

Remind yourself that there are different people who look amazing and who have each feature you have. The only difference is that you have each of those together. This makes you unique and also attractive.

2. On your list, take an inventory of your best qualities.

Some people will have stunning eyes, others hair, or maybe it is their body shape that is stunning. We do not all have to have the same attributes to be attractive. We each have features that set us apart and make us attractive. Take time to take a critical look at yourself and list what is attractive about you.

You can give yourself an image boost by planning a photoshoot that brings out your best attributes. Look at such positive photos often. Remind yourself that it is not that the camera captured a nonexistent you; it is that you have not memorized that you are indeed attractive and amazing. Everyone can benefit from a series of flattering photos and an afternoon of image-booting photography. Be your own best model.

3. Decide on points of self-improvement.

Self-care and grooming are important areas of your self-image. You can develop a list of things you want to work on, keeping a healthy and realistic view of what is possible for you and what is not. If you feel that your body is too tired and sluggish all the time, take on a fitness practice. A fitness practice is anything that captures your interest and is readily available to you.

There is no point in saying you will go to the gym three times a week when the gym nearest to you demands a complete shift in your weekly schedule and heavy financial investment. Such drastic changes will cause you to self-sabotage. Maybe there is a yoga class near you. Whatever you can do without excessive pain and shifts in your weekly schedule will work well for you.

4. Develop a list of personal self-affirmations.

If you have a problem with your body image, you probably also have negative things you tell yourself when you stand before the mirror or any time you think about your body. Listen to what you say to yourself and develop better ways to speak to yourself about your body. Be careful about using any of the insults or slurs that could have been used on you by a caregiver who meant to hurt you.

5. Trash the desire to compare yourself negatively to others.

You are not them! It is that simple.

Take time to list your strengths and abilities, and then keep affirming those abilities to yourself. Develop a list of daily affirmations and read through them loudly or silently at least twice daily; when you wake up and just before you go to sleep.

Remember, if you need to work with a therapist, ask for help. If your self-image is deeply battered, you may need a helping hand. Asking for help is never a weakness.

Chapter Summary

In this chapter, we have introduced specific skills in CBT. The CBT skills discussed can be used alone or with a therapist.

- Go back to the list of social skills. Read through them again and see if you can build that list to 30 social skills that enhance your feelings of self-competence.
- Go through each skill and map your own therapy points. The work will help you to develop a personalized self-therapy model where you work on specific steps towards self-improvement. Remember, self-esteem is not a static metric. Keep working on self-improvement and, soon, you will have made significant progress.
- Build your own standard of attractiveness consciously. Build your self-image consciously. Choose your clothes consciously. Identify your best attributes and enhance those. Your self-image is not static and you can keep improving on it by taking small steps toward feeling better about yourself.

In the next chapter, you will learn about conscious self-reprogramming.

7

CONSCIOUS SELF-REPROGRAMMING

In the last chapter, we discussed CBT skills and how they work. We have mentioned throughout this book the importance of your internal monologue, self-talk, or inner dialogue. Your inner voice contributes to how you see yourself, others, and the world. To shift your feelings of despondency, changing your inner voice is crucial. We also mentioned that to shift your inner critic, you must alter the way you speak to yourself, and it has to be a deliberate and conscious change.

This is because memory is one of the most crucial aspects of your life and your inner critic is domiciled in a part of your memory that is difficult to reprogram. Reprogramming already implies that there is some kind of fixed data that you need to overwrite. This is what you will be doing with the inner critic in this chapter.

LET US TALK ABOUT MEMORY

Memory is a critical aspect of your being. Memory refers to the things you remember, including experiences, hopes, and plans. Memory also helps us to reason, to learn, and to understand. Among your experiences you will store both good and bad experiences. The brain uses a complex process by which it links what you see, taste, touch, hear, and smell to memories. The packets of information are saved and reconnect on demand in the recall process. These information packets are what we experience as memories.

For our discussion, we will only mention two types of memory, short-term memory and long-term memory. Short-term memory is information that we retain for anything from an hour to a couple of days. It also includes the thoughts we are thinking and the things we perceive in the moment.

Information that is required for longer is moved into long-term memory. We retain this information for weeks, months, and even years. A few things enhance the retention of information: emotional stimulus, how much attention you give to the information, your interest in the content, the environment in which you receive the information, and repetition.

REPROGRAMMING THE INNER CRITIC

All the memories accompanied by your internal dialogue have four main functions:

1. To criticize yourself, which includes evaluating and correcting yourself.
2. To support yourself, which includes self-evaluation, self-reflection, development of self-knowledge, self-awareness, as well as giving yourself reinforcement, instruction, and motivation.
3. To manage yourself, which includes grooming, feeding, and self-care.
4. To assess your environment, which includes making judgments about safety, people, landscapes, and the way you interact with all of them.

You, therefore, must not get the impression that internal dialogue is bad or only negative. Neither is the function of criticizing and correcting yourself a wholly negative aspect. What makes it negative is when you run your inner dialogue on a thread that does not see any positives in anything you do.

The purpose of reprogramming the negative critic is to reinforce your ability to give yourself positive commendations. It is also to correct yourself without being condescending. It is to find a new way of talking to yourself that is self-supporting.

AUTOMATIC THOUGHT PATTERNS

If you have maintained an inner dialogue journal like has been suggested in earlier chapters, you will start to pick out certain phrases or certain emotional attachments you are likely to tell yourself on repeat. Repetition is a huge aspect of our learning process and subsequent retention. Think about learning how to write, speak, walk, cook, etc. In all things you do with ease, you had an element of repetition that enabled you to finally carry out the activity smoothly.

This is important in regards to your inner monologue. In time, you can take time to listen to yourself in context. For instance, if you have a fear of public speaking, what are some of the things you tell yourself before you appear before people?

If you keep a journal of these phrases, you will find that you have favored phrases that you constantly repeat to yourself. If they are highly emotive, you can trace the emotional trigger that precipitated the deep internalizing of the phrase or thought pattern.

What you say to yourself on repeat is not just thought, it goes into your long-term memory and becomes habitual thought. Think of learning how to drive. You practice driving until one day it is automatic. You can get into your car and drive without thinking about the process even once.

This is the state called **automaticity**.

According to the online psychology site, Very Well Mind,

"Automaticity refers to skills that, once learned, can be conducted with a minimal amount of conscious thought such as walking, bicycling,

> *driving a car, etc. This particular faculty allows an individual to use their active intellect to deal with other matters."*

— VERY WELL MIND

Think about learning a certain way of thinking in given circumstances so that you leave your cognitive mind to deal with other things. If your habitual inner monologue says, *"I do not like people,"* then without thinking, you will simply be put off by people.

This is why reprogramming your inner monologue is so important. You want your automatic thoughts about important matters to serve your best and highest interests.

Just as it takes time to learn driving, walking, speaking, and other skills where you attain automaticity, learning new ways of thought takes time. Your monologue journal will help you to identify the repeated thoughts that are really hurting your results.

LEARNING A NEW SKILL

To learn a new skill, you start by learning the basics. Then, once you have the major pieces in hand, you repeat them until the brain reaches automaticity.

Learning to think in ways that empower you or in ways that affect your self-esteem takes the same format. First, you think the said thoughts once. Then you add more pieces of the idea to the initial idea. Then you start to repeat these statements until they become an automatic part of your inner monologue.

Also, remember that the brain attaches what you can see, smell, taste, and touch to packets of memory. To retain a memory strongly, you add emotion. In the case of your inner critic, you attached a strong emotion of pain, fear, defeat, etc.

Since you do not wish to recreate the pain, you will purpose your new thought packets as statements that empower you.

This description of negative self-talk from *Psychology Today* captures what we have said up to this point perfectly.

"Negative self-talk is very common. Most of our self-talk consists of beliefs programmed into us when we were children. We heard these beliefs so often, or in such emotionally intense situations, that now we believe them and repeat them to ourselves whenever the occasion arises."

— PSYCHOLOGY TODAY

STEPS TO REPROGRAMMING THE INNER CRITIC

We have already touched on the steps in various chapters, but here we will put the complete system in place so that you can keep coming back to it as your deliberate workbook. The goal is to achieve a definite transformation of your inner monologue.

1. Start listening to your inner dialogue.

As often as you remember to, silence your mind enough to listen and observe the one-man self-argument going on within you. Soon you will start to hear that many thoughts are not really your thoughts. Your inner dialogue is more than just you thinking about your day.

2. Draw up a list of points in your inner monologue.

Listen for the counter-arguments you put out against doing something important to you. Write them down. Develop a **self-talk journal**. List the things you say to yourself as you identify them. Observe them. What attitudes do you hold about yourself? What attitudes does the inner monologue reveal about your view of the world and of others?

3. Ask yourself, "*Is that true?*"

Question the ideas that come up in your inner monologue. Do not accept the counter-arguments that pop up in your monologue as factual or cast in stone. Be particularly keen in questioning the statements against or about your character. "*I am a loser.*" Pick statements like this apart. Who says so? Why do you think so? What facts confirm this? Is that who you really want to be?

4. Watch your body when you get triggered.

Someone commented about your hair and suddenly you felt shame. How did your body respond? Where did you feel shame? In your belly? Did your whole body grow warm? Become familiar with emotional reactions.

When you start to identify your emotional reactions, besides being aware of your inner monologue, you can tell when you are going to react to a conversation, before the emotional response comes through. Your body reacts first.

Have you ever been in a situation where you were about to be hit by something? You will realize that your body responds first. You shield your face. You duck. Whatever response is necessary to shield you comes first and then the cognition of the threat follows. You logically figure why you need to shield yourself a moment after you have ducked. Say someone raises their hand to slap you. You move your face away and intellectually recognize the threat a split second later.

That split-second difference is the difference between being ruled by your emotional responses and taking charge of them. When you feel an emotional response coming on, take a deep breath and count to three or ten, depending on the magnitude of the emotional reaction coming on.

Some emotional reactions will be less violent than others. Counting to three or five will suffice to help you get a hold of your reaction.

5. Consciously and deliberately map a counter monologue.

Go through your most common statements and make a positive counter-statement.

Negative: I never get things right.
Positive: I am willing to learn.

Negative: This is dumb; it won't work.
Positive: Let me try this and see if it works.

Negative: Nobody appreciates me.
Positive: (Make a quick list!) These are the people who appreciate me.

Negative: I am always late.
Positive: It is becoming easier to be organized and to keep time.

Here are additional sentences and ideas of new ways you can speak to yourself to counter the negative self-talk.

- I am not alone. I will find people who can help me through this.
- I know people undergo difficult situations all the time and overcome them. I will too.
- Circumstances do not have control over my responses. I have control over how I respond to situations.
- I am not wrong or weak for feeling this way. Feelings are a way to call me to pay attention.
- Things have worked out before, I trust they will work out this time.
- I have confidence in my abilities, I know I've got this.
- With the right knowledge and resources, this will be something I can accomplish.
- I have no reason to panic or to feel anxious. I will tackle one thing at a time.
- I am confident about my ability to stand up for myself.
- I am confident I can present my side of the story competently.
- I love that I am now more aware of the things going on around me.
- I am paying more attention and feel less overwhelmed by life.

- I am not too in my head anymore.

6. Train yourself never to complete a negative self-criticism statement.

Never complete a negative statement against yourself. End it as soon as you become aware of it. End the statement mid-sentence, if you must, especially when speaking out loud. End it mid-thought. Train yourself to cut off a negative statement and replace it with the selected positive one. It will feel awkward the first time, but in time you will shift the way you speak to yourself. ¶

7. You did not learn to be negative in a day; give yourself time.

Practice these steps for some time. Give yourself three to six months. Watch how your inner monologue changes. Watch how you feel about yourself and about the world around you. Keep giving yourself positive feedback on the slight changes you observe.

8. Become aware of the self-talk of the people you interact with often.

Friends, family, and the people you interact with often influence your perception. If you have people who are negative to themselves, you might want to consider changing your friends or your environment. To begin with, however, just learn to listen and observe and keep your inner counsel. Awareness gives you the power to decide on how to respond. Identifying the problem will help you map out the best solution.

SPEAKING YOUR TRUTH TO YOURSELF

As you carry out your journaling practice, you will discover that you have learned to lie or to speak untruths to yourself. You may not be the initiator of these untruths, but you have been speaking them to yourself often. Make a commitment to yourself to be true. Start with being truthful to yourself. Extend the truth to your conversations with others.

There is a thin line between positive bias and self-empowerment. A positive bias is trying to convince yourself that all things are love, light, flowers, and butterflies, and that everything will always work out well, even when you have not put in the work to raise the chances of a positive outcome.

Example: If you want a healthier and agile body, positive self-talk is in order, but so is a healthier diet and exercise practice. If you want a promotion, self-affirmation is beneficial, but so is taking that extra study, applying for that higher-paying job, etc.

Do not use self-affirmation to dodge the demand for self-improvement. Using positive affirmation as a means to lie to yourself is counterproductive. You will eventually start to mistrust your own voice. Merge your self-affirmation with necessary action.

PRACTICE SELF-EMPATHY ALL THE TIME

We think of empathy as us being empathetic about another person's challenges, difficult situations and experiences. There is a need to be compassionate with ourselves too.

The inner critic discussed in an earlier chapter is you not giving yourself a break. It is you looking at yourself from the harshest possible point of view. You tell yourself that you should have been perfect but are not.

Self-empathy asks: *"But who demands that I be perfect? Is there such a thing as a perfect human being? Who put that standard in place? Do I have to meet that standard?"*

When you demand perfection from yourself to begin with, you plunge back into negative inner monologue. You set standards for yourself that are so high, and then you fall short. When you fall short, you will feel horrible, and then you are back on the treadmill, trash-talking yourself.

Self-empathy means you understand that you have to go through experiences as you do; that some experiences will be difficult. Some experiences will be easy. You will also have all the other experiences in between. Self-empathy means you do not make harsh judgments on yourself that start with such things as "you never" or "you shall never." Avoid superlatives on yourself.

GETTING AHEAD OF HARMFUL THINKING

Life is generally biased towards negativity. We will hear and think about negative reports more than positive ones.

The negativity bias as described in Wikipedia as the notion that

> *"...even when of equal intensity, things of a more negative nature (e.g. unpleasant thoughts, emotions, or social interactions; harmful/traumatic events) have a greater effect on one's psychological state and processes than neutral or positive things."*

What is the *negativity bias*?

The brain reacts more strongly to negative stimuli. Studies done by John Cacioppo, Ph.D., at the University of Chicago found that people viewing pictures of pleasant things such as well-arranged foods, and beautiful landscapes, had far less brain function than when they viewed gory and bloody images.

As a species, we are wired for survival. Our brains, therefore, respond to stimuli that are threatening way more violently than stimuli that are calm and friendly.

This same negativity bias applies to the way you respond to negative things said anywhere in your hearing. You are naturally wired and are more likely to remember the one negative sentence spoken than to remember the thirty positive ones.

Becoming aware of this brain function will help you to go easy on yourself. When you do hear more negative things sooner, that is not an indication that you are wrong and never going to hack this self-esteem thing.

Take an inventory and find what is positive that you could observe in the circumstances. Always ask yourself, *"What positive thing could I learn out of this? What positive outcome could there be out of this? What positive thing I'm I missing here?"*

These kinds of questions will help you to quickly move away from the negative bias that was pulling you down and get back on the pathway of building yourself towards confidence and effective living.

STAYING AHEAD OF YOUR TRIGGERS

When you struggle with low self-esteem, you also struggle with an ever-pulling urge to feel unhappy and dissatisfied with life.

As already discussed, you have had a lot of input to get you to this type of inner monologue. The goal of rebuilding your self-esteem is to help you pull you out of the tendency to be morose and feel worthless. Rebuilding your self-esteem is a method to help you become more inclined to give yourself a reason to give life a more positive outlook.

Your triggers are stimuli that will set you off more than others. You can learn to identify your triggers with precision by monitoring the main conversation of the influencing voices that led you to the negative sense of self.

Remember, sometimes, the inner critic will take the voice or tone of a negative parent, teacher, or an authority figure you met somewhere along your life path.

The individual may have had a favorite sore spot they kept poking. It could be your physical appearance, performance, voice, or achievements. Whatever their pet peeve was, that will most likely be your core trigger spot.

You get hot and bothered when someone compliments your appearance because you learned, *"You are fat and ugly."* This pattern is repeated in whatever your trigger points are. Do you feel triggered when you meet age mates who are doing better than you are? Could this mean you have issues with your performance? Where did you pick that sensitivity from?

What new ways to talk to yourself can you use to boost your self-esteem and your beliefs about your performance?

Triggers are always telling you a story when you pay attention.

Chapter Summary

In this chapter, we have outlined the steps to reprogramming your inner monologue. Come back and review the steps to reprogramming your inner monologue often.

- Develop a ***self-talk journal*** and maintain it for a year. Review it daily as often as you can. Let it be your beacon of light towards changing the way you speak to yourself. ¶
- Identify areas where you are particularly sensitive. Identify why they are such trigger points. Develop definite ways to improve your self-talk in these areas.

In the next, chapter we will discuss managing your external environment.

8

MANAGING YOUR EXTERNAL ENVIRONMENT

Your goal in self-image repair work is to have as much support as possible, and your external environment is a part of that. This chapter offers you specific ideas to handle specific self-esteem areas. How can you map out your self-esteem-building goals?

In this chapter, we will start by discussing how you manage your external environment. We will re-emphasize that awareness of what is happening around you gives you a definite plan on the solutions to consider to build your own self-support initiatives. Awareness of the areas that can be challenging in rebuilding your self-esteem is important too.

Notice so far that much of the work of improving your self-esteem has been internal. In all personal development, much of the improvement work will focus on what is going on within you more than what is happening around you. However, in situations when your environment is negatively affecting your self-esteem and triggers relapses, then it is also important to give attention to your external environment and map out how to change it.

SKILLS TO OVERCOME BODY-SHAMING

Verbal abuse is traumatizing and breaks down self-esteem significantly. In cases of physical abuse, it is not uncommon for the abuser to disfigure their body to give them power over their victim. Remember, the abuser usually has low self-esteem and will do anything to bring their target victim to their level of pain or lower.

If you are a victim of body-shaming, whether accompanied by physical abuse or not, you are aware of all the hurtful things that were said to you about your body. The abuser used terms that made you feel ugly and unattractive.

Body-shaming carries over into adulthood. If an individual has an abusive spouse who attacks them by shaming their body, then the lack of self-esteem is compounded. If body shaming has a physical abuse component, the individual is severely battered around their feelings of unattractiveness.

IMPORTANT: *If you are in a relationship where your partner hits you, whatever their gender, seek the help of a therapist as soon as you can. The sooner, the better. Do not make excuses, do not blame yourself, and do not make yourself an enabler in the abuse by defending the actions of the abuser. Most physical abusers will not stop until they have caused irreparable damage, what they say notwithstanding.* **Seek help as a matter of urgency.** *The same is true if your partner is cruel in their body-shaming remarks. If they are driving you to self-harm habits such as avoiding food, substance or alcohol abuse, etc., please seek help urgently. Tomorrow, too often, is too late.*

Social media and mass media often set standards for how people should look. This makes them enablers to the rather common situation where you can be body-shamed by a total stranger. In cases of cyber-bullying, the people harmed the most by a body shaming assault are individuals who are already struggling with self-esteem issues around how they look. You will meet the regular condescending talker who is insensitive and yet others who will body shame strangers on social media platforms.

How do you deal with these situations?

GETTING THE UPPER HAND AGAINST BODY SHAMING IN SIX STEPS

1. Build a thankful relationship with your body.

Body shaming is tunnel vision in practice. It is looking at just one aspect of your body, maybe weight, height, skin color, etc. at the expense of everything your body is doing and is capable of. It is narrowing who you are to just one aspect of your body. To expand your awareness of your body, do this exercise daily or at least three times a week.

When you will not be disturbed and you can concentrate, take about 10 to 15 minutes to think about all the things your body does for you. Move systematically from head to toe. Your head hosts the brain and the mind. What do those do for you? Let your mind run through all the skills you know are stored in your memory, which is a part of your mind. Think about all the words you know. Think about everything your body does daily from digestion to pumping blood, all controlled by your mind. There is so much good your body does for you.

Now thank your brain and mind as a part of your body that serves you. Feel the gratitude as deeply as you can.

The following day, move to the next item. You could move to your hair, your eyes, your ears, your mouth, your skin, feet, knees, etc. Linger on each part per day and think about all the delightful things that organ or part does and sincerely thank your body for this part and for what it does for you.

The purpose of this exercise is to develop a loving relationship with your body. To move your mind away from what you do not like or what you were body shamed over. It is teaching your mind to see and think about all the other wonderful aspects of your body.

2. Choose your information platforms.

We have already noted that social media, mass media, entertainment, and many such platforms are enablers of making consumers feel unattractive. One of the most persistent messages in advertising of cosmetic products as an example is, *"Without smooth skin you are not good enough."* Or without the white teeth, or straight hair, or specific height, or without whatever else they sell in the advert, you do not measure up to some unwritten standard.

Become selective about your information sources, social media platforms you frequent, celebrities and public figures pages that you follow, etc. If they make you feel "less," then click out.

Become particular about the messages you receive from external sources about who you are and what you are worth. You are much more than a slim form, blemish-free skin, white teeth, etc. Do not allow external voices to make you feel unattractive.

3. Develop self-affirmations about your body.

You had a parent or someone in authority, or an abusive spouse who kept telling you how you do not measure up to a standard of attractiveness because your body is one way while attractive people are another way.

You will have picked up on these repeated words in your inner monologue. Make a list of the ones specific to your body and develop a list of your best attributes. Whenever you are about to say something negative about your body to yourself or to someone else, stop and use the positive affirmation you have already developed. You will find more details on how to do this in the previous chapter.

4. Take time to develop a conscious self-care routine.

Your clothes and your grooming send a very definite message to your brain. If you are feeling on top of things, it translates into feeling better about yourself. Put extra attention to your grooming and self-care routine and stick to it. Rest when you need to. Stay hydrated. Let your clothes add to your feelings of being on top of things.

Additionally, an exercise routine will make you feel much better. You may also consult a food therapist and find ways to boost your energy through diet. Always choose a diet you can easily maintain and one that is in tandem with your beliefs. Food is a means to life. Do not get tempted to turn food discussions into religious practice.

If you were a victim of food-related abuse, build a new relationship with food. Speak to your food, develop an eating pattern that you can commit to. Think about the good things food does for you. You can link these to the body parts exercise. To your brain, think about how energy in the body helps you to remember things better. Read up on food and how it positively affects your body.

5. Change your walking and sitting style.

When you slouch, you send a message to your brain that you are feeling low and tired. Give it a trial. The next time you take a walk, lumber along slowly, looking down at your feet. Then at another time take on a brisk walk and look straight ahead of you. Evaluate how you feel both times.

When you sit, hold yourself up straight, and at another time, sit low in the chair. Observe how both postures make you feel. Adopt the one that makes you feel better.

6. Change your environment to avoid verbal abuse that affects your self-esteem.

From your self-talk journal, identify all the phrases that are a direct attack on your body. Develop a conscious list of new ways to speak to yourself about your body. Move away from negative people. If they are colleagues, step away. Make friends with people who tend to be positive and avoid negative talkers. If they are family, plan to move away from them when you can.

Always remember that seeking help is not a weakness.

COMING OUT ON TOP AFTER CAREER SHAMING

Yes, people shaming people on things that are not their business does not stop at body shaming. Career shaming is a thing. The worst kind of trolling online will be around someone who has had to take a lower job or move lower on the economic scale for various reasons.

Are you a victim of career shaming? Are you a new parent and have had to do something different to find time to be there for your children?

According to the *Working Nation*, men suffer much more humiliation about their jobs than women. "...*Their identity is very often connected with their jobs and job status*." Men connect more with their jobs at an emotional level, while women connect more with their children and family.

A man's sense of self will take a beating if he has to take a lower job. Everyone feels uncomfortable if they are unable to pay their bills comfortably. Many people will respond by being aggressive and hostile, but in truth they are feeling vulnerable and not very confident.

RECOVERY FROM CAREER-SHAMING IN THREE STEPS

1. Find words to express the resentment out loud.

For men particularly, either alone, with a friend or with a therapist, try to put words into what you are feeling and say them out loud. Speak it out loud. For example, "*I resent this situation where I have to take a job that is way beneath my skills, training, experience, and abilities.*"

Men have a harder time voicing their emotional responses to challenging experiences. Once you voice it, you will feel a sense of relief. Relief is an important emotion in working through negative feelings. Through relief, you realize the situation may not be as bad as you thought. Relief opens up your mind to explore other ways of thinking about the matter.

2. Explore alternative ways of looking at the situation.

As discussed in an earlier chapter, listen to what you are telling yourself. Observe your inner monologue. What do you believe about earning less? What do you believe earning less says about you? Is it true? Find better ways to speak to yourself about the situation.

3. Find friends or other people to speak to.

Remember, your self-esteem drops and with it, the disinterest in activities that you previously enjoyed. One of the things you must avoid is self-isolation. If need be, find new friends. Find a community. Participate in activities of interest to you.

Self-esteem is also a mental health matter.

How well are you managing your mental health in a fast-paced world? Do you wake up and zoom off to the next task?

If you are a new mother or a mother to young children; body changes, excess fatigue, etc. could all significantly affect your self-esteem.

Where do you work? What work do you do? What does your job take away from you daily?

Who is in your life? What do they take away from you daily?

Everyone needs a moment to sit still, at least once a day and just go within. Find that place of inner silence to regroup and remember who you are.

Your wholeness is not in the speed and efficiency of the outside world, but in how well grounded you are within.

Take 15 minutes to just breathe. You can make this a meditation practice and listen to your breathing. Take a deep breath in and then out and just watch your breath. Be deliberate about it —nothing to do. Nowhere to be. Nothing demanding anything from you. If you can perfect this practice, ensure you have a daily moment of inner centeredness, you will find that your mind rests.

Your mental health will be greatly enhanced if you can recharge your inside with such brief moments of silence. At first, it will be second to impossible to quieten your mind for more than five seconds. But with practice, you may even fall into a deep slumber. This sleep rests the mind and leaves you feeling mentally alert.

Alongside all the other practices outlined in this book, this inner grounding will enhance your mental health too.

A WORD ABOUT BUILDING SELF-ESTEEM IN OLD AGE

Self-esteem decreases as we age. To start with, if you had a regular job and then you retire, there is a high possibility that you lose connection with most friends. This alone can lead to feelings of being isolated.

If you didn't have a clear plan on what to do after retirement, suddenly having too much time on your hands can make you feel like you are not contributing to anything meaningful.

Many people develop health complications as they age. This may lead to an inability to do things you were previously quite capable of doing for yourself. This can affect your sense of self.

As we all grow older, life events and new experiences may leave us feeling adrift and unsure of how to handle them. In this section, we will look at suggestions on what you can do to be proactive toward building self-esteem as you grow older.

1. Think about what you will do at least five years ahead.

Much of life does not come to us accidentally, it unfolds gradually. If focus on what you would wish to accomplish in the coming year to five years, you tend to stay motivated.

A plan helps you anticipate age-related changes. Being a parent can take all your attention away from the passage of time. Then suddenly, you find that your children have left home and you are not sure what to do with yourself.

Or you may be busy with life and not notice the retirement years creeping on you. An annual to five-year plan helps you keep an eye on life's major milestones. In that way, they are not too overwhelming when they come around.

2. Take a self-care break.

If you have recently come to a life-changing milestone, take a self-care break. Indulge yourself by redoing your hair, taking a long bath, or do something for yourself that you always wanted to do, but couldn't for whatever reasons. Start an exercise routine. Take up a spiritual boosting habit such as yoga or meditation. Do things that are purely centered on you, just this once.

3. Start a gratitude journal.

A gratitude journal is a daily or weekly journal where you pen the things that you were grateful for in the day or in the past week. Most of the time we feel despondent because we fail to see the good happening around us. We focus too much on the things that are not working.

A gratitude journal shifts your focus on the things that are working. If you develop the gratitude journal as a habit and maintain it for a while, you will soon discover you have more things to be thankful for than you thought.

4. Challenge your mind.

Learning a new skill or hobby is one of the best things you can do to counter your negative self-talk about age. It helps you remember that you can conquer a matter when you put your mind to it. Learning a new skill may also open your eyes to abilities that had always lain latent within you. The change of focus will help you close the gap where you feel morose and unappreciated.

If you take up a new skill where you interact with others, you are united as learners trying something new. You will feel more connected with others. Fumbling is an excellent way to help you remember that life is not always that serious; you can start something new and meaningful at any age.

5. Find ways to connect with your age mates.

If you have common interests with your neighbors, pay special attention to those, especially in groups. You can deliberately seek groups that help you tap into your unexplored interests such as sports, hobbies, travel, etc.

Try and stay connected with old friends as much as possible, especially those with whom you have either history or interest in common. It is more difficult to make new friends as we age. We all go through varied life experiences. They make us think differently about common issues.

Old friends ensure that you, at least, have some areas of commonality in perceptions and views. Do not shy away from connecting with old friends on modern social media platforms. Find ways to stay connected with others with whom you can share meaningful conversations.

If you enjoy such activities as catering to friends and you have the means for it, bring friends together. Host events, and attach them to charity work. Find ways to become useful in your new circumstances. You may also choose to get involved in other volunteer activities where you contribute to meaningful causes.

PRACTICE ASSERTIVENESS

Assertiveness is a key characteristic that you may have lost over time. The longer you have lived with low self-esteem, the less assertive you are likely to be.

Chase Hill, best-selling author, personal growth, and social interaction specialist has several works on assertiveness and how to stand up for yourself. He says assertiveness means"...*that you can act in your own best interests and don't feel guilty or anxious about it. It is a significant change for those who have spent years putting other people's needs and desires before their own.*"

Assertiveness can be very difficult for an individual living with low self-esteem, but you want to recover that ground. As mentioned elsewhere, you want to be able to say "*yes*" when that is the relevant response and the one that works best for you. You also want to be able to say "*no*" when that is the best response for you and that is beneficial to your overall well-being.

Being assertive is crucial in relationships, work, and all areas of life. Without assertiveness, people are likely to steamroll you. Some will do so deliberately because they can. Others will do so quite unwittingly because they were not aware of your preference or interest.

Assertiveness enables you to negotiate win-win agreements. In a personal relationship, you may not want the same things as your partner in a given situation. Is there a way to express yourself calmly, in clear words, so that you both come to a resolution that will make both of you happy? Think about that.

Win-win negotiations happen everywhere; at home and at work. Your ability to speak your mind clearly means that for the most part, life will be fairly pleasant for you. You will get desirable results, and where you do not, you will know what to do to get to them. In some situations, letting the matter go is part of being assertive. You will not need to accuse yourself of being useless or incompetent. You will accept that we all win some and lose some and that is alright.

Being assertive will help with various challenges, including social anxiety, depression, lack of interest in things that are important, substance and alcohol abuse, and in our particular context, low self-esteem.

There is also a balance between assertiveness and being pushy and disrespectful of other people's wishes and preferences. That is why the negotiation aspect of assertion is so important. You want to be fair, even as you are not ceding ground that you know you really should not give up.

So if assertiveness is such an attractive character trait, how do you develop it?

1. Learn to listen before you speak.

Most people listen to respond. You can train yourself to listen and understand. When people feel heard, they are more likely to be amenable to a point of view that is different from what they initially wanted.

2. Learn to ask for what you really want.

Take a deep breath, think through your words, and state what you want as clearly as possible. Life will often surprise you because most people will agree with your request. More often than not, you only need to ask.

3. Remind yourself often that you deserve the good that life has to offer.

We have given a lot of attention to your inner monologues throughout this book. You deserve the good that life has to offer. You are not an underdog who takes the crumbs. Make this part of your reframing and reprogramming exercises. It will help you to ask for the things you really want and deserve.

4. Speak with your body language.

Staring at your toes, shuffling along, slouching in your seat, avoiding eye contact. All these are ways to say, *"I am not sure of myself."* If you struggle deeply with communication and body language, a body language and image consultant will help you develop the best non-verbal ways to be assertive in communication.

5. Decide on your boundaries in advance.

If you are walking into a negotiation, decide what you can accommodate and what is completely unacceptable. Be aware of your boundaries before you start a conversation. That way, you will not be caught off guard agreeing to something you did not want. If you are caught off guard, remedy the situation as soon as possible. Within 24 hours is a good window. Go back to the person and renegotiate.

6. Train yourself to appreciate the good that others do.

Just like learning to listen, being appreciative of what others do and their successes will make them more amenable to hearing you out when you have a matter to discuss.

Chapter Summary

This chapter gives you plenty of practical steps to help you rebuild your self-esteem.

- To come out on top from body shaming, build a new relationship with your body that is different from the one you were taught to believe in.
- To overcome career shaming, work your way through the shame until you can find new ways to think about the situation. There possibly is something grand about your new circumstances.

- To rebuild your self-esteem as you grow older, and through life-changing circumstances, take time out for yourself, have a plan on the things you want to accomplish, stay connected with others around you.
- Assertiveness will win you many milestones in life that you always thought were unattainable. Most of the time, asking is the only thing standing between your desire and its attainment. Ask.

We have come to the end of the *CBT Skills & Practices Workbook for Self-Esteem.*

You have plenty to build on to develop and maintain your sense of self, confidence in your abilities, and assurance that you deserve the good things in life.

Fighting low self-esteem is a lifelong battle. If you have ever broken a bone, you know that you favor that limb for the rest of your life. If you have ever gone under the knife, no matter how perfectly the operation went, and how perfectly the wound healed, you know that there is a moment you cannot bend just so. You prefer movements in a way you did not before.

Healing and building battered self-esteem is the same way. Although you will look and talk as everybody else, you will always have points of sensitivity where your mind will respond in ways that are just so. You will know that you have certain vulnerabilities in circumstances that others will not notice.

Healing is one thing. Knowing you have your vulnerabilities and that is absolutely normal is another. If you are a victim of physical abuse, you will always be the person who has a higher sense of unease in particular circumstances. This is your self-preservation's way of keeping you safe. It is not a weakness. It is not a bad thing.

If you have had challenges in your relationship with food, you will always be the individual who will take an exceptionally long breath when you walk into a room set with a lavish buffet.

Understanding this about yourself is an important aspect of staying away from relapses. Part of the reason we relapse into old patterns is that we tell ourselves we were never that person with a problem. We slip into unawareness. We tell ourselves that we are so healed that there is no remnant of the damage. That does not make you a winner, it makes you vulnerable in dangerous ways.

Well, if your self-esteem challenges were mild and fleeting, you may have little to almost no lasting damage. You can completely revert to your previous self where your self-esteem was not a problem. However, if your self-esteem was battered from childhood and was compounded by various experiences as a teenager, or if you experienced even more problems in adulthood, the tendency to revert to feelings of worthlessness will always linger just below the surface.

That is what makes you victorious. The knowledge that you have overcome life hurdles that most only dream about. This vulnerability does not make you weak. It makes you courageous and stronger than most people in the room at any given time. Above all, it makes you wiser.

You faced difficulties and overcame them; that is what heroes are made of.

Taking steps to improve your self-esteem. Asking for help. Working with yourself or with a therapist to improve your self-esteem, will not erase the years you had challenges. Those will always be part of your learning experiences. They will be a part of who you are, going forward.

What working on yourself to improve your self-confidence will do, however, is to help you become more comfortable with yourself in all aspects of your being. You will be more accepting of yourself. You will see yourself more objectively. As already mentioned, you will become a better friend to yourself, and that is the best gift you can offer yourself.

The practices offered in this book are therefore not hit and run ideas that you will use for a few days and then put aside. This book is a life manual. It is a lasting companion. It is a friend that speaks to you, reminding you that there is a better day ahead.

Your inner monologue took a long time to craft. You are working on rebuilding ways to speak better to and about yourself each day. Teaching yourself to both listen and speak to yourself in constructive ways will be one of the most diffi-cult things you will ever handle. The mind has entered into a thinking habit. Habits are difficult to break.

Therefore, do not work on your self-talk journal for a couple of days, decide you now have the idea mastered and stop the practice. Keep this workbook close and come back to it often. As soon as you feel yourself slipping back into old thought patterns, take out the workbook and remind yourself of the things you have learned.

The most important thing to remember is never to shy away from asking for or finding help. Asking for help is the way of the courageous and the victorious. It says,

---

"I see the magnitude of the challenge I am facing, and I am confident enough to say, 'I need a hand.'"

Congratulations for doing exactly that by picking up a book that shows you ways and practical skills to build and rebuild your self-esteem.

Life-changing events can and will shake anyone's foundations. That is not a sign of weakness. It means you have lived life and have battle scars to show for it. Deaths, for instance, tend to rattle even the best of us really badly. The difference between coming out of the experience, coping well thereafter, and being plunged into depression lies in being courageous enough to ask for help.

Separations, divorces, children leaving home and moving on with life, losing a job, retirement, the onset of a difficult health condition, finding yourself in an abusive situation you never anticipated, or loss of important contracts that set you back significantly on your economic plan; life happens.

Few things in life follow a script that we can confidently say we were certain that the events would unfold in a particular way. For this reason, you must not be too hard on yourself when faced with difficult circumstances. Do not make difficulties your fault.

It is also the reason you should not shy away from seeking help. Whatever you are facing, you do not have to go through it alone. Find help.

If you feel overwhelmed by all the changes you have to deal with— whatever those changes might be —remember, seeking help is always a good thing.

There are options for both paid and free therapy. An online search will reveal what is available in your vicinity.

There is a heavy emphasis on your inner monologue throughout this text. It is deliberate. Nothing shakes your world outside than your world inside. If you can master your inner monologues, you will have mastered a great deal in your outer world.

It is the key to better relationships, better jobs, previously unattainable achievements, and better results in everything you set out to do. Positive inner monologues separate people's life experiences in fascinating ways.

For instance, the one who always says, *"I am always late,"* will for some reason miss the bus on important days. Their means of transport will be terribly delayed on a most inconvenient day. There will be unexpected weather that completely disrupts their schedule at the worst possible time.

On the other hand, the one who has learned to say, *"Things work out in my favor all the time,"* will find that, in fact, things strangely work out in their favor. They are the people generally called *"lucky."* They have learned that they are the masters of life and the key is in how they choose to think about life, themselves, and their environment.

Your world is waiting to give you support as you improve your inner monologues.

As you come to the final words in *CBT Skills & Practices Workbook for Self-Esteem,* make a decision to pick a journal and make your new practices habits. They will serve you well and for a very long time.

Welcome to a new life using CBT skills to build your self-esteem.

REFERENCES

Books

1. Beck, Aaron T. "Cognitive Therapy and the Emotional Disorders." Plume, October 1, 1979.
2. Dr. Mattke, Angela C., M.D. "Mayo Clinic Guide to Raising a Healthy Child." Mayo Clinic Press, April 16, 2019.
3. Helmstetter, Shad, PhD. "What To Say When You Talk To Your Self." Amazon Kindle, Jun 9, 2011.
4. Ramachandran V. S., MBBS PhD Hon. FRCP. "Encyclopedia of Human Behavior, Volume 2." Academic Press, May 2, 1994.

5. Gillihan, Seth J. PhD. "Retrain Your Brain: A Workbook for Managing Anxiety and Depression." Sheldon Press, July 23, 2020. ¶

6. Maslow, Abraham H. "A Theory of Human Motivation." Amazon Kindle, January 16, 2011.

7. McKay, Matthew, PhD (Author), Fanning, Patrick (Author), Vance, Gillian (Narrator). "Self-Esteem: A Proven Program of Cognitive Techniques for Assessing, Improving, and Maintaining Your Self-Esteem." New Harbinger Publications, August 7, 2019.

8. Buchalter, Susan I. "Raising Self-Esteem in Adults." Jessica Kingsley Publishers, January 21, 2015.

9. Wilding, Christine. "Beat Low Self-Esteem With CBT." Teach Yourself, December 19, 2017.

10. Martell, Christopher R. "Behavioral Activation for Depression: A Clinician's Guide." The Guilford Press, January 4, 2022.

11. Linehan, Marsha M. "DBT® Skills Training Handouts and Worksheets." The Guilford Press, October 21, 2014.

12. Maltz, Maxwell. "The Magic Power of Self-Image Psychology, 2nd Edition." Prentice Hall Direct, November 1, 1989.

13. Hill, Chase. "Assertiveness Training: How to Stand Up for Yourself, Boost Your Confidence, and Improve Assertive Communication Skills." Kindle Books, November 10, 2020.

Dictionary and Encyclopedia

1. The Macmillan Open Dictionary
https://www.macmillandictionary.com/dictionary/british/persuasion?q=persuasion+

2. Wikipedia, the Free Online Encyclopedia
https://en.wikipedia.org/wiki/Main_Page